图书在版编目（CIP）数据

兴国老别墅 / 走走文字．—上海：上海科学技术文献出版社，2012.11

ISBN 978-7-5439-5537-0

Ⅰ．①兴… Ⅱ．①走… Ⅲ．①别墅—介绍—上海市 Ⅳ．①K928.8

中国版本图书馆 CIP 数据核字（2012）第 209855 号

责任编辑：王 珺
装帧设计：许 菲

ISBN 978-7-5439-5537-0

兴国老别墅
文字 走 走 摄影 何璐璐 翻译 陈向普
出版发行：上海科学技术文献出版社
地 址：上海市长乐路 746 号
邮政编码：200040
经 销：全国新华书店
印 刷：上海书刊印刷有限公司
开 本：787×1092 1/16
印 张：12.75
字 数：201 000
版 次：2012 年 11 月第 1 版 2018 年 12 月第 3 次印刷
书 号：ISBN 978-7-5439-5537-0
定 价：78.00 元
http://www.sstlp.com

目 录
CONTENTS

香樟树局部特写
close-up of the camphor Tree

在香樟树下，听上海老洋房讲故事
The Tales of the Old Villas Under the Camphor Trees

“海纳百川、兼容并蓄”的海派文化，因其多元与多彩，不知吸引了多少人驻足凝视。人们的流连，同时也成就了海派建筑文化，小道梧桐、洋房木梯，造就了中西合璧、艺术交融、风格独特的老上海建筑特色。

Due to its ongoing diversity, Shanghai continues to attract and hold the attention of the world, which in turn makes possible the uniqueness of old Shanghai architecture. The streets, the buildings, the avenues of platanus acerifolia, the villas behind the garden walls make Shanghai unique, where the architecture of the west and the east meet, and melt together as one.

老上海的历史，浪漫中不失典雅，精致中带有神秘，让人神醉痴迷其中；而老上海的建筑犹如张爱玲所说的30年前的故城月色，让人追忆回味。如果想了解老上海的历史，那么，让我们去听听老上海的老房子所讲的故事吧。

The history of Shanghai from the late 19th century into the early 20th century, makes the city romantic, elegant, sophisticated as well as mystical, and leaves one intoxicated and enchanted. The architecture of old Shanghai, just as Zhang Ailing remembered about the moon in her hometown some 30 years before, makes one nostalgic, The tales of the old houses and villas of Shanghai continue to bring that history back.

兴国路是一条幽静的马路，在上海市区西部，为长宁、徐汇两区界路。北起华山路，南至淮海中路。长799米，宽15.2米，车行道宽9.0米。民国九年（1920年）后填浜筑北段，民国二十一年筑南段，以法国公董局秘书的名字命名雷上达路。民国三十二年以“江西兴国”改今名。

The tranquil Xing Guo Road is located in the west of the city, serving as the demarcation line between Chang Ning and Xu Hui districts. Starting with Hua Shan Road in the north and ending with Middle Huai Hai Road in the south. The northern part of the road was paved in 1920, by filling in the river, and the southern part was carried out 13 years later, named Route Remi after the secretary of Conseil d'Administration of the time, in 1944, it was renamed after Xing Guo, Jiangxi Province and used today.

在夜晚，沿着这条静谧的马路前行，路灯被梧桐树叶遮得有些昏暗，却似乎更能洞悉上海的精神。兴国路是宁静的，静得有些沉默，有些低调，所有引以为傲的一切，都被砖瓦收藏了起来。从20世纪初至今，多少年过去，砖瓦已然黯淡，建筑却依然散发着它昔日的光辉。一栋有故事的建筑，已经超越了建筑本身，与这些陈年的故事在此邂逅，从砖瓦中读出情怀，从历史里品味典雅。

Walking along this quiet road at night, with the street lamplights rendered dim by the branches of the ancient plane trees, the quiet Xing Guo Road is modest, with all of its pride locked up in the pages.

有120年树龄的葱郁香樟树
the 120-year-old camphor tree

Since the beginning of the 20th century, the building still radiates its former glory. A building with a story is more than the building itself. To meet the story here and now, one can read through these pages and to understand the city better.

著名的涉外五星级酒店兴国宾馆就坐落于这历经繁华的马路北端，78号。这里位于上海市领馆区的中心，拥有得天独厚的地理位置，延安路高架近在咫尺，车行至虹桥国际机场仅15分钟，至浦东国际机场55分钟，至徐家汇商业中心仅5分钟。出行购物、饮食娱乐都极为方便。78号大院占地面积13.33万平方米，建筑面积2万多平方米，几乎占据了兴国路、华山路和湖南路三条马路相围的全部土地。在20世纪初，这里是洛云浜西侧的农田，1932年租界当局修筑了雷上达路以后，外国洋行陆续在此建造别墅，均由洋行大班居住。

The celebrated international five-star Xing Guo Hotel, lies right on the northern tip of the street, at No.78, placed within the centre of the former consular district, with the Yan'an elevated highway a mere 30-minute drive to Hong Qiao International airport, and a 55-minute drive to Pu Dong International Airport with 10-minute drive to the commercial centre of Xu Jiahui, along with shopping, food and entertainment districts are all easily accessible. Covering an area of 133,300 square meters and floor area of more than 20,000 square meters, the entire compound occupies the majority of land at far end corner of Xing Guo, Hua Shan and Hu Nan roads. At the beginning of the 20th century, the area was originally fields west of Luo Yun river. After the Concession authority built Route Remi, in 1932, foreign companies succeeded one another in building villas within the compound, serving as the residences for their Taipans.

对大多数上海人而言，兴国宾馆即便在今日依然是一个有些神秘的地方。这份神秘感也许是源自20 世纪50 年代，毛泽东和他的最后一任妻子江青曾居住于兴国宾馆一号楼，而今兴国

❧有120年树龄的广玉兰
120-year-old magnolia

❧有100年树龄的大王松
100-year-old pine tree

宾馆的八号楼亦是上海市领导人会晤重要外宾的最高规格接待场所之一。

Still today to a majority of people in Shanghai, the Xing Guo Hotel carries with it some mystery. This mystery might be attributed to the fact that as early as 1950s, Xing Guo Hotel Villa One was home for Mao Zedong and his wife, Jiang Qing. Today Villa Eight set within the centre of the compound is a leading venue, where summit meetings between the Shanghai Municipal leaders and foreign dignitaries are held.

身处其间，如同徜徉在近代上海建筑风格的博物馆：从早期英式风格的独立花园住宅，再到中西合璧造型及装饰艺术风格……历史被错落有致、呈环形地加以展现，不是用语言，而是用建筑。兴国路78号大院内除一号楼外还有两幢上海市优秀近代建筑保护单位，即兴国宾馆二号楼、六号楼，分别建于

1925年和1922年。这三幢风格各异的欧式别墅建筑，是兴国路78号大院内13幢别墅建筑的一部分，其中一至六号楼为太古洋行建造的专供洋行高级职员居住的花园别墅，分别按照英国、德国、法国、美国等国的建筑风格建造。

When walking through the grounds, one has the impression that you are visiting a museum with the array of buildings, ranging from the early European style along with British influenced garden style houses, architecture combined Chinese and Western styles, or of Art Deco style. Apart from Villa One, another two notable buildings Villa Two and Villa Six which were built in 1925 and 1922 respectively, and have been listed by the Shanghai Preservation Department. These three European style villas are part of the 13-villa complex within the main Xing Guo compound, amongst which are Villa One and Villa Six by Butterfield & Swire, for their senior employees with references to the architectural styles of Britain, Germany, France and America respectively.

走进兴国宾馆，满眼一派欧洲园林风光。花园里，大树参天，绿草如茵，静谧幽雅，绿意盎然，百年老树随处可见。林木深处坐落着一幢幢红白各色、风格不同的西洋小别墅，充满异国情调。甫进入大院，就使人有远离城市喧闹、身临城市森林之感。

Walking into the grounds, one might be surprised at the expanse of garden that greets you. Wherever you look, your eyes are met with rolling green grass and towering trees. Here you find hundred-year-old trees are of no rarity. Right there in the depth of the woods, lie a number trees and plants. One escapes the intensity Shanghai beyond the walls of Xing Guo in this calming green environment.

多少动人故事曾经在兴国宾馆上演，今时今日，故事的主人公们早已远去，这些美丽的别墅群却依然故我，犹如一个个凝固了的旧时梦境，我们还能在此体验故事里的生活方式。品一口红茶，耳闻花园中鸟鸣声声，青草的香气萦绕身畔。你可以向每一个“兴国人”打听这里的历史，他们会向你娓娓道来，那一段悠长又伴随着温暖的传奇。

The Xing Guo Hotel has been staged many a moving story over the years. Today, with the characters long gone, the buildings are just like old dreams made still and timeless, allowing one to catch a glimpse of the past and to savior the former lifestyles, Perhaps a sip of tea, with the singing of the birds and the fragrance of the grass in a garden setting.

香樟树下的石凳，据说毛泽东早年曾在此读书
The stone seats and table under the camphor tree. It is said that Mao Zedong used to read here.

一号楼：最有历史和故事的老洋房

Villa One: The House with History and Many a Tale

兴国路78号

78, Xing Guo Road

1994年被列入上海市优秀近代建筑，市级文物保护单位

Listed by the Shanghai Preservation Department in 1994 as an Historic Site.

一号楼全景图

a panoramic view of Villa One

兴国宾馆内有一幢气势不凡的建筑，那宽敞的平台及高大的楼层与周围的别墅相比，显得格外醒目。这别具一格的宅邸就是由世界建筑大师克列夫·威廉·埃利斯爵士设计的一号楼，也是兴国宾馆内最出名的一幢花园洋房。

Villa One is in itself an imposing building and a contrast to the surrounding villas, its spacious platform and tall floor render it striking. This unique building, is the most well known garden villa which was designed by Sir Clough Williams-Ellis.

一号楼是现在兴国宾馆内唯一一栋完整保存的洋房。大半个世纪的洗礼并不能减弱这座华丽豪宅的魅力，尽管时光将其原来的紫铜屋顶染上了片片铜锈斑驳的淡绿色，几乎被周遭香樟、梧桐的丰润绿色“掩藏”掉。在凭高远眺它时，再也看不到当年屋顶金灿灿的场景，但这反而更与四周的百年苍翠相得益彰。

The beauty and charm of the building has not waned, despite being some 70 years old, though time has rendered the originally copper roof into verdigris green, which is in harmony with the surrounding camphor trees and platanus acerifolia trees.

一号楼位于兴国路78号大院内，是英商太古洋行大班的住宅，建于1934年，原名“赫世屋”，为何特地取了和一幢当时位于涌泉路、静安寺路（今天的延安西路）上19世纪60年代建的房子一样的名字，已经成为一个谜团了。现为兴国宾馆一号楼，也叫“小白宫”，是上海新古典主义建筑的杰出代表，建筑面积为1,647 平方米，两层砖混结构。

Villa One was built in 1934 and intended as the residence for the Taipan of Butterfield & Swire. It was originally named Hazelwood after a house built in 1860s on the Bubbling Well Road （West Yan’an Road today） with an unknown reason. Now it is the Villa One in the Hotel, also known as the Small White House. It is the representative of Shanghai Neo-Classicism architecture, a two-story brick building with a floor area of 1,647 square meters.

多少年来，一号楼见证了数不清的历史事件：起先是太古洋行，这是一家曾经在相当长时间内垄断中国航运的英国商行；新中国成立后，这里又成为市委办公厅招待处，后来又更名为兴国招待所……无法计算这里曾接待过多少位国家领导人，毛主席、周总理都曾多次在这里下榻，直到现在，它还

❧一号楼老照片 early pictures of Villa One

❧一号楼老照片
an old picture of Villa One

是兴国宾馆最重要的外事接待场所之一。

Over the years, the building has witnessed countless historical events: first was Butterfield & Swire, a British company that once monopolized the Chinese shipping business for a number of years; the founding of new China saw it changed into the reception of the General Office of Municipal Party Committee, later into Xing Guo Guest House. Countless state leaders have been accommodated here, such as Chairman Mao and Premier Zhou who had been here upon more than one ocassion. Until now it is still one of the most important reception sites for foreign guests in the hotel.

中国营业公司打造的“太古圈”
The Swire Circle Created by China Realty Co. Ltd.

在新中国成立前，延安东路和延安中路分别叫做爱多亚路和福熙路，再以前它们则分别是叫做洋泾浜和长浜的两条相接的河流。这两条河就是上海公共租界和法租界的分界河，河的北面是公共租界，河的南面则是法租界。1900年，法租界的西界在白尔路，就是今天的重庆中路，1914年法租界扩张成功，今天华山路以东的地区全部被划进了法租界新界。而中国营业公司初建时，静安寺以西的沪西尚未划进租界，租界外的土地大多是农田，地价相对低廉。而雷文熟知上海的土地行情及规划，他知道，当这些农田被划进租界后，就成了城市用地，地价便会即时攀升，这个有头脑的商人将眼光瞄准了那些农田，以较低的价格购进土地进行开发。

Before 1949, East Yan'an Road and Middle Yan'an Road were called Avenue Edward VII and Avenue Foch respectively. Shanghai International Settlement and Shanghai French Concession were separated by the Yang Jing Bang, a creek flowing into the Huang Pu River, which was later filled-in and became Avenue Edward VII, and is now Middle Yan'an Road. In 1900, the western border of French Concession was Bell Road, which is known today as Middle Chong Qing Road. In 1914 the French Concession succeeded in expansion and the area east of today's Hua Shan Road was added to the French Concession.

与公共租界相比，法租界的商业和经济都落后不少，法租界公董局的税收不足，可用于新租界开发建设的资金实在有限。于是当这块新租界刚到手时，法租界公董局便出台了相应的措施，支持和鼓励开发新租界的各种商人和商事机构。中国营业公司主要是通过以下两种方法参与法租界的房地产经营：一种就是直接投资，即由公司先自行出资征购土地，对原农田进行平整、改造，在该土地上兴建住宅，使土地升值后再以高价出售或出租。当他们购进一块相当面积的土地后，就请设计师将土地划成若干块，并通过经租人到各大公司游说，鼓动公司买房，住宅可以由客户自己委托设计，也可以由中国营业公司设计；另一种即房地产中介，以中介身份代客购地建房。他们先对愿意出租、转让土地的业主调查登记，再由他们寻

❧一号楼一楼长廊
the corridor on the first floor

找想租用、购买土地的下家，公司收取中介费用。兴国宾馆的部分住宅是属于前一种方式，所以今天兴国宾馆内的多幢别墅，都是由该公司先期购进地皮后兴建的，这里的地产也是由中国营业公司经营的，但每幢建筑都有着鲜明的个性。由于房子造好后大多出售给了太古洋行，于是兴国宾馆的地块旧时被叫做“Taikoo Circle”，中国人则称其为“太古圈”。

Compared with Shanghai International Settlement, the business and the economy in Shanghai French Concession lagged far behind. With the insufficient tax income, the money available for the development of the new area was very limited. Thus with the newly acquired land,

the Conseil d' Administration introduced a policy to support and encourage businessmen and institutions to develop the new area.

太古洋行大班从未住过的豪宅
The Villa Which the Swire Taipan Never Lived in

太古洋行的总部设在英国伦敦，远东总部设在上海，统管中国、日本、南洋各地的业务。上海太古洋行的办公楼位于繁华的法租界外滩，洋行的管理者——大班则选择居住在幽静的法租界西部，他的地位类似于今天的跨国公司驻华首席代表。由于上海在太古洋行的亚洲战略中占据着重要的地位，太古洋行除了在上海设主管，具体负责上海公司的业务外，总部还派董事会董事定期或不定期驻上海，监督上海的业务进展，并对重要业务或重大事件做出决策，所以高层领导均常年居住在上海。在斯维尔的儿子、人称小斯维尔的乔治·斯维尔（G. W. Swire）接管太古洋行、执掌公司大权时期，他决定为高层领导在上海挑选合适的地块修建专门的住宅。

With the headquarters in London, Swire made Shanghai their headquarters of the Far East, taking charge of the businesses in China, Japan and Southeast Asia. The office building of Swire in Shanghai was located on the Bund in Shanghai French Concession, while the Taipan chose to live in the more quieter part of the concession. The Taipan would be a chief executive of a multinational company in today's terms. Due to the importance of Shanghai, in Swire's Asian strategy, apart from establishing a manager specifically in charge of the business in Shanghai, the company also sent board directors to Shanghai on a regular basis to monitor the companies business and to serve as the decision makers. The key executives lived in Shanghai all the year round. When Swire's son, G. W. Swire, known as Swire

❧一号楼一楼卧室 bedroom on the first floor

❧一号楼的会客室 reception room of Villa One

Junior was at the head of the company, he decided to find an appropriate area to build residences especially for the key managers.

20世纪30年代，爆发了一次世界范围内的经济危机，这场始于美国华尔街的经济危机使当时作为远东金融中心的上海也无法独善其身。据历史资料记载，仅1934年，上海民族资本企业就倒闭了425家，失业队伍日益膨胀。与此同时，经济危机的爆发也给一些有远见的资本家找到了低价购地的良机，小斯维尔就是其中之一。

1930s witnessed a worldwide financial crisis. This crisis started in America, and Shanghai being a financial centre in the Far East, was not spared. It is recorded that in 1934, 425 national companies in Shanghai closed down with the unemployment rate soaring every day. During this time the crisis provided the best chances for the visionaries to buy land at very competitive prices, with Swire Junior being one of them.

由于当时太古在中国的业务日趋多元化，也使得公司能够堤外损失堤内补，即便在全球经济危机背景下，集团财力依然雄厚，这才使得一直对上海房地产市场雄心勃勃的太古经理们下定决心，趁着廉价劳动力充足的时机在市中心大兴土木，建立一个奢华总部大楼，也就是今天兴国宾馆的一号楼。小斯维尔看中了中国营业公司的一块位于沪西雷上达路、海格路、朱尔典路（今兴国路、华山路、湖南路）相围的土地，并以高价购进了这块土地，修建了数座别墅建筑。

Due to the companies diversified businesses in China, Swire even during the financial crisis were able to survive and thrive. This gave impetus to the managers of Swire, who have always been able to seek opportunities in the real estate market within Shanghai, hence, the construction of Villa One in today's Xing Guo Hotel. Swire Junior, fixed his eye on the land where Route Remi, Avenue Haig and Route A. Charles 'Culty met. He purchased the land at a high price and thereon built several villas.

1934年，对于上海建筑行业来说，是个奇妙的年份。这一年，百老汇大厦（现在的上海大厦）竣工营业；同年，扬子饭店（现在的朗廷扬子精品酒店）开业迎客，也是这一年，现在的兴国宾馆一号楼建成。

1934 was a legendary year for Shanghai as far as architecture was concerned. It was in this year that Broadway Mansions （now the Broadway Mansion Hotel） was completed and open to the public; it was in the same year that Yangtze Hotel （now the Langham Yangtze Boutique Shanghai） opened for business; it was also in this year that the Villa One was completed.

1941年太平洋战争爆发后，太古洋行的英籍职员作为敌对国难民被遣返回国，洋行产业则作为敌产被日伪接管，别墅也被日本军方占据。第二次世界大战中，太古洋行在沪经营活动大受影响。抗日战争胜利后，1945年，太古洋行重新收回了产业，发现主卧室里已经赫然建成了一个榻榻米房间。

After the Pacific War broke out in 1941, British employees of Swire’s were either lucky enough to escape or interned into concentration camps. As a result, the company was taken over by the puppet regime, and the villa occupied by the Japanese Imperial Army. World War II took its toll on the business of Swire in Asia and China, Swire were able gain back its businesses in 1945 after the victory of the Pacific War, and to Villa One again.

一号楼水晶门把
the crystal doorknob of Villa One

战后太古洋行的贸易虽有所恢复，但未能重返长江航运。那时，太古洋行上层已估计到中国内战爆发在即，中国的生意以后不会太好做了，所以决定逐渐缩小投资，这栋豪宅就被变卖了。其后，蒋介石曾将许多重要活动和会议安排在这里。

Although the post war era saw a recovery of the business for Swire, but the former days of glory were over, especially with the impending civil war on the horizon. Business in China could no longer regain the previous momentum. As a result, the company divested, and Villa One was sold. Later on the villa became the venue for a number of important meetings and activities arranged by Chiang Kai-Shek.

❧一号楼一楼会客厅里的留声机
a gramophone in the reception room of Villa One

毛泽东、刘少奇等曾在此下榻
Accommodation Once to Mao Zedong and Liu Shaoqi

上海解放后，这栋洋房被市政府军管会接管。1952年以后，上海第一任市长陈毅等领导在此居住。1956年划归新成立的上海市委办公厅招待处，初时仅简单定名为“上海市委第一招待所”，许多中央领导人到上海均入住此宅。后又改名为“兴国招待所”，名字虽然仅叫“招待所”，从服务到设施却始终保持高标准、严要求，因为当年“兴国招待所”主要接待的都是由北京来沪出访的中央领导。毛泽东、刘少奇、朱德、贺龙等老一辈无产阶级革命家都曾在此下榻。

Following the liberation of Shanghai, Villa One was taken over by Military Control Commission. In 1952 and the years to come found the villa home to Chen Yi, the first mayor of the new Shanghai. In 1956 the building was placed under the newly established General Office of Shanghai

一号楼的方形棚屋老虎窗
the squared-shaped dormer of Villa One

Municipal Committee. The building was simply named as Guesthouse Number One of Shanghai Municipal Committee, which received many state leaders. Some time later, the building's name was changed to Xing Guo Guesthouse. Though named as guesthouse, it adhered to strict criteria ranging from the service to the facilities, as it mainly accommodated the state level leaders from Beijing. Mao Zedong, Liu Shao Qi, Zhu De, He Long all resided at the property one time or another.

现在英国和香港等地太古公司的员工如果来上海，都会要求入住一号楼，有些企业文化寻踪的意味。只要那时没有政府领导下榻，兴国宾馆还是很乐意接待他们的。

When Swire employees from overseas visit Shanghai these days, they always ask to be accommodated in Villa One, as if going back to their roots. The Xing Guo Hotel is always willing to accommodate their request.

英式古典建筑
British Classical Architecture

一号楼是座充满浓郁文艺复兴风格的大班住宅，堪称建筑师运用柱式手法表现建筑严谨、端庄、气派的成功作品，帕拉第奥母题在这座建筑的设计中表现得淋漓尽致。正面南立面分左、中、右对称的纵三段。底层是外廊式风格，采用多立克式双柱，柱顶是圆形，上有方石盖顶，凸出的半个柱廊有“浮雕”的效果。柱廊后为落地钢质玻璃统长门窗，处理简洁典雅，这一别致的廊式设计风格主要受欧洲近代建筑中注意室内外空间联系的影响。即墙内建有宽敞的内廊，廊侧才是房间，这样的话，炎炎夏季，内廊可隔离火辣辣的阳光，而到了冬季，将廊边门窗关闭，可起到保温的作用。在此之前的大多数建筑中，柱廊的两端是封闭的，但帕拉第奥提出了一个新的设想，将封闭的墙也改为圆拱的窗，无形之中增加了建筑的空间感和立体效果。既可以增加建筑的牢固，又增加了建筑的情调。

The imposing two-story building has a greenish copper roof which slopes to the west and east sides. The building is concise, elegant yet luxurious. The outside walls are whitewashed with the whole building presenting a classic structure of three longitudinal sections and three lateral sections. The building is composed of the main building and the parallel auxiliary building. The plane of the main building corresponds to the facade, emphasizing the symmetry of the axis. The main building faces the south with a northern entrance. In the east there is a single-storied house attached to the main building. In front of the mansion is a balcony and vast expanse of lawn and grounds, the auxiliary building is linked

一号楼外宽阔的草坪 the lawn outside the building

一号楼阁楼楼梯
the attic stairs

with the pantry in the east wing of the main building; as a result, it doesn't affect the appearance and light of the main building. A curve is fashioned in the part where the protruding part in the north and the main building meet. In this way, it not only corresponds to the curve-shaped vehicle lane but also creates the effects of the distinction between the main and the attached annex.

可能为了强调视觉的变化，建筑师在二楼外廊采用了宽敞的爱奥尼克双立柱柱廊，柱头上卷起特有的旋涡状装饰，让直线条多了几分优雅和情趣的内核，回廊宽敞通透，并以宝瓶式栏杆围护。后面棱角方正的阳台是凹进式的，背面入口处的雨篷轮廓近似立方体，以粗壮方形柱墩转角，每面柱墩间各立一对多立克式柱。

❧一号楼老照片
an old picture of Villa One

Probably for the visual change, the designer used double Ionic order in the corridor on the second floor, with scrollwork at the top which renders the straight lines more graceful and entertaining. With the bottle-shaped railing, the corridor seems spacious. The square-angled balcony is recessed with the cube-shaped awning at the back and the square pilasters at the corner, between which there stand a pair of Doric columns.

论述外国古代建筑史的专业书籍认为，多立克适用于各种与基督教男性圣徒有关的建筑；爱奥尼则用于女性圣徒、文人高士的建筑；科林斯用于圣母玛利亚；混合柱式用于凯旋门、建筑最上一层。这些不同柱式，在兴国宾馆都可以见到。

According to books specialized in the architecture history of the West, Doric is usually applied to the buildings connected with Christian bravery and apostles; Ionic usually seen in the buildings concerning female saints and intellectuals; Corinthian is linked with Madonna and composite order is applied to Arc de Triomphe and the top floor of a building. All of these diversified classic orders can be found in the building.

一号楼建筑外观上最特别的地方要属屋顶。当

一号楼长廊 upper floor corridor

时，它的屋顶使用了数十吨重的紫铜板，经年累月地就生成了一层厚厚的铜锈。所以，现在的屋顶呈淡绿色，一号楼也就因此有了“铜顶楼”、“铜房子”的别称。

The most striking about the building is the roof. In the very beginning, the roof was built with dozens of tons of copper plates, but time has rendered it crusted. Therefore, with the greenish roof, Villa One was nicknamed “the building with the copper roof ” or even “the copper house”.

建筑主入口设在主楼北面中央，挑出宽大的门廊，两边是车道。主人下车后沿着台阶通过小门厅进入楼梯厅。大门廊和小门厅地面均用大理石铺设。楼梯厅平面是椭圆形，东侧设弧形的大楼梯，西侧设弧形走廊，连通卫生间。靠壁大楼梯是楼内的一道亮丽风景线，随着角度和距离的变化，出现了一幅幅不同的画面，这大概就是人们常说的步移景换吧。

The main entrance is set in the middle of the north side of the main building with a large porch, the floor of the porch along with the entrance hall is paved with marble. Alighting from one’s car, the owner walks up the stairs into the reception hall. Once inside you are greeted by a large painting of the building, a large sweeping curved staircase.

一号楼建筑内部空间简单实用，清晰明了，井井有条，楼内设有起居室、卧室、餐厅、会客室、台球室、吸烟室、儿童房等大小不等的15个房间。穿过楼梯厅进入大过厅，过厅东面设餐厅、西面设台球室，还特地辟一小间为吸烟室。过厅南面大间为会客室、小间为起居室。主楼南面设宽敞的柱廊，连通各房间。弧形大楼梯由于层高较高，设半平台。二楼宽敞的过厅连通各个房间，南面两间卧室，中间为卫生间，可从其穿通。东面是由起居室、卧室和卫生间组成的一套主人房。西面为两间卧室及合用卫生间的儿童房，并在墙外挑出了统长阳台。房间之间有走廊和楼梯相连，南向的卧室外面都连通宽敞的柱廊。坡顶下的三层为储物室。

Villa One has both a simple and practical interior, orderly and neat. There are altogether 15 rooms, including a sitting room, bedrooms, dinning room, meeting room.

楼梯前东西贯通的长廊使室内显得格外宽敞。在北立面入口处二楼的上方屋顶山花部位有一个椭圆形玻璃雕刻装饰图案，周围花饰细腻纤巧，属典型巴洛克时代设计风格，站在这里，可以感觉到阳光和阴影跳动的变换，对一号楼建筑整体的立面起到了画龙点睛的作用。整幢室内装饰带有文艺复兴风格，显得简洁、典雅、气派。

The furnishing within the villa are of a renaissance style simple, yet elegant.

辅楼的底楼为厨房，南面设一条短过道，通过台阶连通主楼备餐间，这样可以减少厨房对主楼的噪音。采用一个直跑小楼梯上楼，二楼为佣人房。

The first floor of the auxiliary building is the kitchen, with a corridor on the south leading to pantry in the main building through a flight of steps. In this way it can reduce the noise of the kitchen for the main building.

该建筑的主立面朝南，设计师在秉承英式皇家古典风格之时，还借鉴了意大利文艺复兴时期的"广场式"设计。从二楼的任何一间房间都能通往巨型阳台。这片阳台正面对着一个足有几十亩、像足球场般大小的一片绿茵草坪，两侧严格对称，使住宅掩映在各种名贵树木花卉之中。院内树木长青，四季花香，在近百种树木中有江南仅存的两株大王松和百年老香樟、五针松、塔枫、雪松、龙柏以及银杏、香榧、金橘等果木，景色幽雅，环境怡人，能让人享受到安静的园林气氛。

The main facade of the building faces south. Whilst inheriting a classical British style, the designer borrowed ideas from the square design of the Italian Renaissance. Each room on the second floor leads to a large outdoor balcony that faces the lawn with both sides being in perfect symmetry, with the house set among a variety of valuable trees and flowering shrubs. Amongst which is a surviving platanus acerifolia, a hundred year old camphor tree, white pines, maple towers, cedars, Chinese torreyas along with kumquat trees.

The appealing environment makes one intoxicated with this tranquility and garden aura.

满屋子的传奇故事
A Houseful of Tales

这座设计、施工精良，得到较好维修保护的新古典主义建筑的代表作

❧ 一号楼餐厅
the dining room

品，1994年被列为上海市优秀近代建筑保护单位。

This well-preserved masterpiece of Neo-Classicism design with its perfect design, fell under the Shanghai Superior Modern Protected Buildings act in 1994.

据说，修建此楼的那位太古洋行的巨头——老板小斯维尔仅在建筑竣工时来过上海一次，参加了竣工剪彩仪式后即返回英伦，从未在这栋豪华宏伟的住宅里住过一天，他的目的是“将它建成一件城市景观”。看来，伦敦的生活非常舒适，他也就再没有过住到上海的念头，从此再也未曾来过上海。这栋豪宅名义上的户主是太古公司伦敦总部派驻上海的首席执行官G. E. Mitchell。不过落成后，这里曾长期作为太古洋行总部办公楼使用。每逢年过节和重要的纪念日，太古洋行的高层都要在此进行社交活动和举行商业会议，出入太古洋行总部的亦非富即贵。所以这里没有按传统的别墅设计，而是参照了有公共空间的广场设计。建筑内宽大的扶梯与内廊，与其说是住宅，还不如说是公共图书馆更合适。一号楼门前的大草坪也是当年上海滩上流社会豪华派对的首选场地。

It is said that the tycoon of Swire who constructed the villa, Swire, Jr. came to Shanghai only once at the completion of the villa, and he returned to Britain right after the completion ceremony. Intending to make it a landscape in Shanghai, he never lived a single day in the

一号楼二楼卧室
the bedroom on the second floor

house. Obviously, life in London was so cozy that it never ever occurred to him to live in Shanghai. In fact, he never came back, G. E. Mitchell, the CEO in Shanghai sent by the headquarters in London was entitled to the ownership of the villa. Yet the completion found that it became the office building of the Swire headquarters. Observing holiday's and important anniversaries, the management executives would hold activities and business meetings. For this purpose, the villa was built in accordance with the design of squares with public space instead of the traditional villa design. With the spacious staircase and the inner corridors, it is more a public library than a residence. The lawn in front of the villa used to be the first choice for both cocktails and garden parties.

一号楼的设计是在克拉夫·威廉·埃利斯爵士与小斯维尔先生每月来往于伦敦和上海之间的信件中完成的，其中既包括了建筑外观和内部配件详细的图纸，也包括石膏装饰、涂料样品和内饰调色。进度报告和照片则每月从上海回传给建筑师。可以说，这栋华丽的一号楼，其实是建筑师遥控设计，和小斯维尔先生共同紧密配合完成的建筑大作。最初建成时，这幢楼还包括一个英式玫瑰园和一个日式花园。正门口左边墙上的一块小铜牌上，可以看见这位建筑师的大名。·

Clough Williams-Ellis completed the design of the house and its interior decoration and these detailed drawings of exterior and interior fittings, plaster casts of moldings and paint samples for the interior color scheme and sent these were sent via mail to Shanghai. Progress reports and photographs were sent back to Williams-Ellis from Shanghai each month. He worked in close co-operation with Swire Junior. At the time of completion, the building also included an English style rose garden along with a typical Japanese style garden. A copper plaque can be seen on the left hand side of wall at the entrance has the designer’s name engraved.

因为这座建筑风格独特，设计精湛，使用者又颇具地位，所以堪称是沪上顶级洋房。当年毛主席来到上海，据说都下榻此处，利用率从此才得到了大幅提升。The villa, due to the unique style, the terrific design and the distinguished residents, deserved to be best house in Shanghai. It is said that Chairman Mao lived here, when visiting Shanghai.

值得一提的是，如今事过境迁，但一号楼依然保持百分百原貌，内部现有的10套客房基本都维持了原样。壁炉、灯具、墙角线等都是以前的老物什。步入明亮开阔的前厅，再沿精雕细作的环形楼梯拾阶而上，透过圆形天窗放眼眺望，随处可见建筑学上均匀

一号楼壁炉
the mantel piece of Villa One

❧一号楼二楼走廊
alter table on the second floor

平衡的美感。而长期以来作为接待国宾、外宾的专用别墅，所能触摸到的红木家私、水晶门把、彩绘灯具、素雅墙纸，莫不散发着历史的味道。大半个世纪的洗礼并不能减弱这座华丽豪宅的魅力。

Time seems to have stood still with the style of the ten suites, being brought to their former glory with the quaint style of year.

如今，门前大草坪上遮天蔽日的两棵香樟树越长越高、越长越大，扎西拉姆·多多写的那首《班扎古鲁白玛的沉默》里有这样几句诗“你见/或者不见我/我就在那里/不悲不喜”，说的也许就是这两株大香樟树。它们历经百年依然郁郁葱葱，正对大楼，树冠尤其葱茏饱满，远看像个大圆球。这两棵香樟树颇有些自由散漫的架势，特别是右边的那株，主树干并不是一枝独秀式的笔直，而是自然发成了四五棵，喝醉般地向外长长地伸展着，树下最适合有情人私密的约会。曾有考察此处的植物学家断言，兴国宾馆一号楼门前的香樟树如今已是全亚洲最大香樟树。

Today the two shading camphor trees on the lawn are growing taller and bigger, and the lines from Zahiram Dodo’s poem *The Silence of Vadjra Guru Pema* might

❧院内四季常青的树木
the evergreens in the yard

be the perfect depiction about these two trees: "You see, or not see me, I'm still there, without sorrow without happiness." Standing right in the front of the villa for a century, they are still thriving and flourishing. Looked afar, the dense crowns seem like big balls. The trees seem to be at great ease, in particular, the one on the right, whose stem is not thrusting straight into the sky, but growing at its own will into four or five branches that stretch far out like drunks, providing a perfect trysting place. Botanists ever surveying here asserted that the two camphor trees before the Villa One were the giants in Asia as a whole.

每逢香樟树开花的季节，空气中多了些浅甜、幽微的暗香，雾气一样缥缈，人在树下，就像被施了魔法，身处一个绿色的梦里。透过斑驳的树影打量这栋

一号楼二楼柱廊 the colonnade on the second floor

❧一号楼的铜板屋顶
the cooper roof of Villa One

白色别墅，犹如梦境。满屋子的故事年复一年地沉积着，日久弥香——

“上海第一医学院附属卫生干部学校设在兴国路一座豪华漂亮的花园洋房里，那是个闹中取静的好地方，环境幽雅，院内树木森森、绿草如茵，有足球场般的大草坪，还有一个游泳池。看到的这一切真叫我一时难以置信，对我这个曾经是上海街头的流浪儿来说，这一切绝不是梦，是确确实实的存在……1953年，上海夏天的天气热得邪乎，既不刮风，也不下雨，身上衣服总是汗湿的，要不是班上还有女同胞，我们肯定会光着膀子在教室里‘开夜车’。幸好，校园里有一个游泳池，热得实在熬不住了，大部分男同学跳进游泳池里游泳……在游泳池里嬉水打闹，轻松快活，凉快一阵子，再出来鏖战数理化！”

In spring there is the sweet fragrance hanging in the air,

which you get by standing under the camphor trees, you might feel enchanted and imagine yourself in a field of green. Looking at the villa through the tree line, you have the illusion that you are in a wonderland. Even now the house still functions as the accommodation to the state leaders when visiting Shanghai.

这是时任周恩来专职保健医生张佐良在回忆周总理的书中提及自己在“华东卫生干部学校”的一段往事。张佐良在1965年至1976年间，担任周恩来的保健医生。文中提到的“卫生干校”，便是这栋一号楼。张佐良也是在此走上了大学路，一号楼自然成了张佐良记忆中美好的一段。

1949年上海解放后，新成立的“华东卫生干部学校”，于1952年通过上海市房管局向当时在法律上仍

拥有一号楼产权的英国房产代理，租借一号楼办学。鉴于一号楼建筑本身在法律上当年仍属于第二次世界大战中的英美同盟国财产，上海市政府亦不能强行征用，怕引起不必要的外交风波。当时一位上海官员想出一条“妙计”，即由上海市房管局向英国代理收取远高于普通房租的特别地税，原因在于一号楼属于历史建筑，需要特别花费保护，由此一来，特别地税远高于英国代理向卫校提出的租金，最终在迫使英国

❧一号楼天花吊灯
the ceiling pendant lamp of Villa One

房产代理向上海市房管局递交了请求房管局代管的报告，于是华东卫校在未花一分钱的情况下，“名正言顺”地拿下了一号楼。

Following the liberation of Shanghai in 1949, the newly formed East China Health School requested to lease Villa One from the British real estate agent who legally owned the house through the Shanghai City Housing Authority. With the building itself belonging legally to the Allies during World War II, the municipal government could not take it by force for fear of causing unnecessary diplomatic crisis. One of the officials hit upon the idea, that the Shanghai City Housing Authority levy a special land tax, much higher than the rent with the reason that Villa One

一号楼天花吊灯
the ceiling pendant lamp of Villa One

从一号楼二楼俯看一楼一角
sweeping view of the entrance hall and staircase

being an historical building needed special upkeep. As a result, considering the tax to be much higher than the rent proposed to the school, the British agent was financially forced to submit to the Shanghai City Housing Authority a Property Entrusting Application report. Therefore, the school were able to take over the building without paying.

1953年，上海市政府计划对一号楼另作他用，于是华东卫校从一号楼迁出。

In 1953, the school moved out of the building as the municipal government needs were greater.

陈毅元帅之子陈小鲁仍然记得自己儿时住在一号楼里的故事："那时候，我家住在上海兴国路上的一座小楼，现在好像是家宾馆。我印象中，父亲很忙不太管我。我早上经常不起床，有时到中午吃饭都不起床。有一天，他不知道因为什么发脾气，吃中饭时又听说我还没起床，一下就急了。他冲上楼，说：'养这孩子有什么用啊？'抱起我，就要往楼下扔。当时把秘书们都吓坏了，也真就把我睡懒觉的毛病治好了。后来我一直早起早睡，到现在都保持着这个习惯。"

Chen Xiaolu, the son of General Chen Yi, still remembered the story that happened during his childhood when he lived at Villa One: "My family then lived in a small building on Xing Guo Road which is now a hotel. I recall that my father was often very busy, I stayed in bed very late in the morning, sometimes till lunch time. One day my father was in a bad temper for some reason. When he learned I had not got up yet at the lunch table, he rushed upstairs, shouting: 'What's the use of raising the child', picked me up and was about to throw me out of window. His act threw the secretaries into panic and cured me of my bad habit. From then on I kept the habit of going to bed early and rising early till this day."

而时任华东局第一书记兼上海市委第一书记的柯庆施也曾在这里疗养过。柯六六在回忆爸爸柯庆施在上海的岁月时这样说道：

Ke Qingshi, then the General Secretary of East China Bureau and that of Shanghai Municipal Party Committee also lived here for some time. Ke Liuliu, his son, recalled the time when his father was in Shanghai:

一号楼拐角辅楼
the auxiliary building

“1964年6月初，爸爸出院了，手术后需静养，依照组织上的安排，爸爸住进市委招待处的兴国路一号楼。这是一栋欧式的老房子，过去我常随父母到这儿来看望聂荣臻伯伯等来沪的客人。爸爸身体虚弱，不便爬楼梯，住在楼下朝南的一间房间。我们四个孩子每个星期天去看望他。几个月来，妈妈完全忘记自己病弱的身体，陪伴着爸爸。日夜的操劳和担忧、紧张使她比过去更显消瘦了。爸爸出院后病情不稳定，发过烧，犯过心脏病。在他出院的第三天就开始发

❧一号楼进门大厅
the entrance

烧，医生诊断他患了流感。持续的发烧使爸爸筋疲力尽。爸爸的抵抗力很差，我们去看望他时，只能站在阳台上，从玻璃窗外向他招招手。党中央安排爸爸去北戴河休养。海边的空气和气候对他养病有利，同时也是让他离开上海，以便安心静养。行程定在1964年7月14日晚7点。7月14日大妹妹考中学，爸爸等她考完试，全家同行。7月13日下午，孩子们来到兴国路与父母团聚。那天气温很高，爸爸说晚饭就在草坪上吃饭吧。爸爸生病住院的三个多月以来，我们全家第一次吃团圆饭。晚风习习，全家围坐在餐桌前。爸爸微笑地看着孩子们，心情十分愉快。晚饭很简单，绿豆粥加馒头。但那是一次令我难忘的晚餐：爸爸的身体渐渐好了起来，全家人又能围坐一桌了。

"In early 1964, father was out of the hospital. He needed recovery following an operation and it was arranged that he move into Villa One, which served as guesthouse of Shanghai Municipal Party Committee. It was an old house of European style and I used to accompany my parents there to visit the guests coming to Shanghai, such as Uncle Nie Rongzhen."

晚饭后，市委办公厅在住处为父亲放映电影。爸爸没有拒绝这一安排。他很高兴地一手牵着小弟，一手牵着小妹走出客厅。宽大的过道，被服务人员布置成临时放映室，搬出一套沙发，面前竖起一方雪白的幕布。放映了一部国产新片，由著名电影表演艺术家赵丹主演的《青山恋》。我曾担心爸爸的身体能否坚持坐上一两个小时，爸爸看完了整部片子，看完之后他问我们，好看不好看啊？当然很好看啦！能和爸爸一起看电影，太好了！……"

"文革"期间，从1967年1月开始，张春桥、姚文元就把他们的"行宫"设在了这里，忙不迭地接见《文汇报》、《解放日报》的造反派代表。十年动乱风云，很多幕后操纵，正是在这里密谋策划的。

During the Cultural Revolution, Zhang Chunqiao and Yao Wenyuan set their headquarters at the property from January 1967 and received several representatives from Wenhui Daily and Liberation Daily. Much of the upheaval during the Cultural Revolution was probably both plotted and controlled here from the property.

现在兴国宾馆一号楼的服务秉承着VIP式原则，以超五星的标准来打造10间客房，而其接待客人也维持着VIP式的挑剔：客人需要至少提前一个星期预定，别墅一体出租，且不欢迎仅仅前来一掷千金的豪客。这种看似非市场

化的管理，除了本着保护老洋房文物的角度出发，也进一步固化了兴国宾馆厚重的文化气息。

The service which one receive when staying at Villa One today, is truly unobtrusive and caters to the needs of visiting dignitaries from near and far.

❧绿树簇拥着的一号楼
Villa One surrounded by the trees

二号楼：纯净的英国乡村气息

Villa Two: A Typical English Style Country Home

兴国路78号

78, Xing Guo Road

1999年被列为上海市优秀历史建筑

Listed as Shanghai Outstanding Historical Building in 1999.

二号楼玻璃窗
the stained glass ceiling

兴国宾馆里坐落着不少异国风情浓郁的欧式别墅，它们悄然隐匿在幽幽绿荫之中，弥漫着神秘的气息，就像一个个世家子弟，带着以往岁月沉淀出来的骄矜和遗世独立的清高，透着骨子里的贵族气。而兴国路也从20世纪20年代传统的自然乡村，到西方人周末乡村别墅区，逐渐形成了鲜明的乡村别墅式风貌特征。

Still today there are a number of villas within the grounds of the Xing Guo, some concealed amongst the trees and foliage.

兴国宾馆最让人惊艳的是这里的绿，它们大片大片极奢侈而炫耀地绽放着，十几栋小洋楼散落在肆无忌惮的绿色里，鸟儿在树丛间鸣叫，营造出一种怀旧而清新的氛围。虽然宾馆里有很多别墅，但并不紧凑，而是相互疏远，不仅为建筑物提供了呼吸的空间，也使别墅主人的私密性得到了保护，而且每一栋别墅都拥有自己独立的花园，若隐若现地露出精心侍弄过的草坪。

The most unforgettable thing about the Xing Guo Hotel and its grounds is the striking green, released in abundance and luxury without any reserve. Scattered among the unavoidable green with birds singing in trees, these villas make for a nostalgic feeling. Though they are many in numbers, these villas are estranged from each other, providing the breathing space for the buildings as well as protecting the privacy of the residents. Every villa has its own independent garden, showing now and then a glimpse of the well-attended lawn.

温馨浪漫的人文气息
Warm and Romantic

兴国宾馆二号楼地块原址是在今天的兴国路靠近华山路处，原海格路695号。海格路，是华山路在1921年到1943年之间的路名，是为了纪念1914年任英国远征军司令的英国将领道格拉斯·海格。当时的海格路，是上海公共租界工部局越界筑路之一，用来抵御太平天国从西面的进攻，也是上海法租界西面的界限。海格路北起愚园路，南至徐家汇贝当路（今衡山路）。一直到1943年10月，汪精卫政权接管租界后，才将这条路更名为华山路。全长4,320米的海格路上，当年沿路都是高级住宅区，花园洋房和高级公寓很多，是美英侨民和中国上层人物的主要聚居地。蔡元培故居、周璇住过的枕流公寓、李鸿章后人的旧居丁香花园……而这座二号楼当时太古洋行规定为上海行政副主管住宅，长期居住者是主管罗克（W. H. Lock）。

Villa Two was built at 695 Avenue Haig, which is today the at the junction of Xing Guo and Hua Shan Roads. Haig, the name for Hua Shan Road between 1921 and 1943, was named in commemoration of the British General, Douglas Haig, commander of the British Expeditionary Force. Avenue Haig, the west border of the French Concession, was built by Municipal Council of the Shanghai International Settlement to resist the attack from the Taiping Rebellion from the west. It runs in the north with Yu Yuan Road and ends in the south in Avenue Petain （Heng Shan Road today）. It was not until October 1943 when the Wang Jingwei regime took over the Concession, that the road was renamed into Hua Shan Road. The 4,320-meter-long Avenue Haig, lined with senior neighborhoods and garden villas and was the residential district for foreigners. The Former residence of Cai Yuanpei, Brookside Apartment, and Lilac Garden which was the former house of the descendants of Li Hongzhang are all found here. Villa Two, intended as the residence for the deputy manager of the Butterfield & Swire in Shanghai, was long inhabited by W. H. Lock.

二号楼是一套英国乡村式假三层砖木结构花园住宅，建造于20世纪20年代。这是一座自然环境与建筑艺术完美结合的作品。它坐落在兴国宾馆的草坪和树木丛中，保存依然完好，外表已经十分陈旧，但门窗却比较新正，墙体映衬着绿色，隐约可见，又别有洞天。英国乡村的形式可以追溯到大约1,500年以前，撒克逊人砍掉森林，以一片草地或一个水塘为中心作为定居地，这些村庄就自发地从教堂或庄园开始发展，随后村舍和花园也因地制宜地建了起来。

Villa Two, a three-storied brick and timber garden residence, was built in 1930s. It is a building that perfectly combines the nature with the art. Situated among the trees and lawns of Xing Guo Hotel, the villa was kept pretty well. Though the exterior is obsolete, the doors and windows are comparatively new. The villa, with

the walls set against the green, is very appealing. The English Country-Style can be traced back to 1500 years ago when the Saxons cut down the trees to build a settlement around a lawn or a pond. The village naturally developed from the church or the plantation and later on cottages and gardens were appropriately set up.

英国给人的大体印象是一个相对保守的国家，比较重视传统和社交礼仪，讲究社会分级和贵族情调的生活，这从英式别墅的建筑风格也可以得到印证和反映。

The English strike people as a conservative nation that respect tradition and courtesy, particularly in social hierarchy and noble life. All of these can be proved by the architectural style of the villa.

欧洲的文艺复兴运动，除了对思想的启蒙和人性的解放外，更影响到社会的各个层面，建筑也不例外。风行于

❧二号楼全景
a panoramic view of Villa Two

18世纪的英国佐治亚风格，便是由意大利文艺复兴风格传入英国后派生出来的，它在英国形成并随英国人的足迹而流往世界各地。

The Renaissance in Europe, besides the enlightenment and the liberation of human nature, also had an impact on every aspect of social life, with architecture being of no exception. Georgian Style popular in the 18th Century appeared after the Italian Renaissance came to Britain and it followed the British throughout the world.

英式别墅在风格上秉承古典主义对称与和谐的原则，强调门廊的装饰性，注重细节的处理，营造一种华丽精致的形象气质，体现的是一种优雅尊贵的生活方式。

The English villa, adhering to the classical principle of symmetry and harmony, stresses the decorative function of the porch and emphasizes the details. Therefore, it creates a delicate image and a noble lifestyle.

在具体的表现形式上，英式别墅常以古典门廊、有齿饰屋檐、分割的细小窗格等作为"门面格局"，并以侧山墙、四坡屋顶、中央山墙的建筑形态出现，多为城市住宅。

The English villa finds expression in the classic porch, the dentil cornice and the finely divided window panes. Moreover, it is mostly used in urban residence in the form of side gables, hip roof and the central gables.

此外，在此基础上发展起来的亚当风格，则是延续了佐治亚风格的大部分，只是在局部做出微调，使之更为精致且更具装饰性。而传统的哥特式建筑、巴洛克风格在英国扎根、生长，并与各种建筑风格相互调谐，左右着传统建筑的走向和新流派的形成，他们共同代表着英国传统建筑精神的高贵潮流。

The Georgian Style-based Adam Style, inheriting most of its predecessor, made some adjustments in details, making it more sophisticated and more decorative. The conventional Gothic and Baroque architecture thrived and determined the future and formation of new styles. Together they embodied the trend and spirit of traditional English architecture.

二号楼的建筑面积是800平方米，维多利亚滨海建筑风格，散发着温馨浪漫的人文气息。南立面一、二层为连续卷廊，二层弧形卷廊有清水红砖图案，顶部并列一大一小、一前一后两个三角形山墙，露黑木构架。西山墙接一层建筑，机制平瓦陡坡屋面。

The seaside Victorian-Style Villa Two, with a floor area of 800 square meters, radiates a warm and romantic humanistic aura. On the southern facade is the overhang of the ground and the second floors, with red brick patterns on the curved overhang of the second floor. At the top, there are two different-sized triangular gables with blackwood frame, one in the front and the other in the back. The west gable, linked with the first floor, is a combination of flat tile and slope roof.

在英式别墅的外立面上，砖木结构的建筑散发着历史的厚重和自然的质朴，单纯的外形、三角形屋顶、精细斜网窗格、精致大烟囱、简单的装饰是其建筑的主要特点，充分体现着原味自然、格调质朴的乡村生活气息。其外墙多用粗砖、碎石或特有的黏土砖，而且大多是砖木结构。如果不仔细观察，很难区分新旧别墅的差别，特别有历史感和沧桑感。二号楼的南立面就是由双坡屋面山墙和一个四坡屋面歇山顶组合而成，山墙及歇山部分用垂直黑色细木条装饰，二层为两组三个清水红砖弧形拱券，窗边饰以清水红砖齿形装饰，底层有九个开间的拱形柱廊，每间均有券心石，透出一种往日岁月的悠悠情韵。

On the facades of English-Style villa, the brick and timber building tell of history and nature. The main features, expressed in the innocent shape, the triangular roof, the windowpanes, the exquisite chimney and the simple furnishing, reflect the country life close to nature. The exterior walls were built with rough brick, rubble and special clay bricks and were usually of brick and timber frame. As a result, it is not easy to distinguish the old from the new, giving the villa a sense of history.

浓郁的英式田园之风
Strong English Pastoral Style

二号楼整个建筑高低错落。外观古朴、典雅，不追求光鲜亮丽。室内木质大梁相互交错，颇有英国乡村建筑原始质朴的田园风味。英式别墅的楼层大多数采用木地板，踩上去“咯吱”作响。为什么英国人喜欢用木结构和木地板呢？估计与英国人的居住传统和习惯有关，也可能是因为木头比较保暖和舒适，不像钢筋水泥那么冰冷、刚硬。

Scattered high and low, the whole building seems simple and elegant. The timber beams inside the building are interlaced with each other, rendering it identical with the English country buildings. The floors of the English villas are usually of wood and stepping on it produces the creak sound. Why do the English prefer the wooden framework and wooden floors, perhaps it has something to do with their tradition and habits, or it might be that wood is much warmer and cozier than the hard and cold steel and concrete.

家具则采用曲线的形式，凸出装饰和复杂雕饰，既舒适，又显得华丽。这些家具都是大尺度的，是展示身份的象征。底层立面整个以灰色为基调，以水平横线条与建筑上部分开，建筑立面活泼、丰富、沉稳、新颖，加上屋面穿出的三座三孔和单孔烟囱及北立面半圆形玻璃墙楼梯间，整座建筑显得豪华、生动，不失为一座优秀的近代建筑。

Furniture in the building is all curve-shaped to feature decoration and complicated carvings, making the furnishing comfortable and gorgeous. Large-sized, this furniture serve as symbol of the status. Grey in keynote, the base of the facade is separated from the upper part with horizon lines. Lively, staid & novel, the facade, together with the three three-holed and single-holed chimneys as well as the glass staircase in semicircle on the north facade, makes the building stand out in modern architecture.

据说，英式别墅的客厅不一定放在楼下，但厨房大多设在与后花园相连的一楼。这是因为英国人虽然没有法国人那么讲究烹调和美食，但对生活也是十分讲究的。他们的厨房就像客厅那么大，是每日三餐和下午茶的场所，可以和家人、朋友享受在优雅宽敞环境下聚餐，或者节假日在后花园烧烤的乐趣。英式厨房至今仍然保留着古典之风，带有弧线的面板、木刻的繁花、斑驳的漆面，以及少量的藤编用品都是古典厨房的特征。英国人的厨房大多连接花园，所以良好的采光是田园风格的关键。此外，手绘彩盆、陶质壶或罐都可以提升厨房的田园之气和典雅的艺术格调。

It is said that the parlor in English-style villa is not always on the ground floor,

二号楼门廊 the porch

❧二号楼玻璃窗
the glass window in Villa Two

yet the kitchen is more often than not set on the first floor linked with the back yard. This is probably because the British, though not as fastidious about cooking and food as the French, are particularly fastidious about life itself. As large as the parlor, the kitchen is the place where they have the three meals and the afternoon tea. They enjoy the time with their friends in this spacious space or the pleasure of holiday barbecue in the back garden. The English kitchen still maintains the classic traits today, such as the curved panel, wooden carved blossom and a few canes. English kitchen is usually linked with the garden; therefore, the good lighting is the key to the pastoral style. In addition, hand-painted basin, ceramic pot or jar can promote the pastoral aura and the artistic touch.

英式别墅的后花园一般都比较封闭和私密，大都用板墙遮挡，外人难以进入和窥视；而前院一般都比较开放、简单，门口也比较窄小，并不特别讲究。花园内则绿树葱茏，芳草萋萋，四时花香，春夏鸟鸣，十分优美雅静。破窗而入的绿色、新鲜的蔬果使田园之风得到进一步细化。

The backyard of an English garden is often closed and private, blocked by boards to prevent access and sight. While the front yard, usually open and simple with a narrow entrance, has got nothing to do with luxury. The luxuriant trees, the green grass, the blossoms and the singing birds make the garden nothing less than a paradise. The green that leap in through the window and the seasonal vegetables and fruits render it more pastoral.

当年不可复制的风情隔着流光款款而来，那种老式的华美奢靡的细节和老别墅竟是如此契合。一切都是静静的，带点儿慵懒，那是老上海特有的遗韵。如今它们像花儿一样悄然开放在繁荣兴旺的兴国路上，兀自散发着暗香。

The luxurious details and the villa match so perfectly, bringing back the beautiful old days. Everything here is typical of old Shanghai, tranquil and a bit lazy. Like flowers, they blossom quietly and fragrantly on the flourishing Xing Guo Road.

英国是崇尚田园生活的国度，从富裕阶层到普通人家对田园的热爱，可以从贯穿在英国文学作品的乡村情结中体现。英式别墅也处处体现着田园风格，与大自然保持亲近。二号楼回归传统，区别于英国大工业时代的繁琐矫饰风格，反映出一种朴素低调的英式田园气息——传统、简朴，尊重生活本义，强调的是别墅对私家庭院的占有和享受，低调而自在。

Britain is a nation that worships all aspects of country life, through all class barriers that is quintessentially. British, their love of nature can be reflected by the country complex that goes through the English literature. The English villa, in every detail, shows its `intimacy to nature. Villa Two signifies a return to tradition. Different from the style typical of the industrialization era, Villa Two embodies a plain and simple pastoral tinge. It emphasizes a respect of life per se and stresses

❧二号楼楼梯 the entrance

the occupation and enjoyment of a private yard.

林语堂曾说，“大同世界的理想生活，就是住在英国的乡村”。这句话不经意间传达出人们渴望回归自然，对宁静、恬淡的英式乡村小镇生活的憧憬。真正的英国乡村生活，不仅是狭义上回归田园、自然舒适的简单生活方式，而是在悠游乡村惬意的同时，能够享受上流社会如赛马、舞会等赏心乐事。当时的几栋别墅都是由太古洋行高层入住，他们尤其喜欢保有私人空间，喜欢独栋住宅，独门独户，三层左右，错落的、舒适的，彼此相见也可以不见。这样的设计，既是实用、习惯，也反映出一种审美需要。走在兴国宾馆里，这些别墅颜色、形状各不相同，足以缤纷有趣，错落有致地散落在那里，辅以园艺，展现出悠游的富贵气度。

Lin Yutang once said that the life in Utopia is to live in English countryside. The quotation unconsciously conveys man’s thirst for returning nature, for the quiet and pleasant life in English countryside. The real English country life is more than closeness to nature or the simple and cozy life style. It means access to such enjoyable upper-class activities as horse race or balls while fully immersed in nature. The several villas there were all for the senior managers of the Butterfield & Swire, who preferred private room and independent houses. The villas, three-storied, cozy and detached, gave them the freedom either of keeping to themselves or of meeting each other. This design is more than practical and habitual, it is a taste. Scattered and set against the gardening in the Xing Guo Hotel, these villas, different in colors and shapes, shine with nobility.

六号楼：经典的法式民居

Villa Six: Classical French Style Residence

兴国路78号

78, Xing Guo Road

2000年被列为上海市优秀近代建筑

Listed as Shanghai Superior Modern Protected Buildings in 2000.

❧六号楼全景 the panoramic view of Villa Six

高贵、浪漫的法式建筑
Noble French Residence

兴国宾馆六号楼是一幢砖木结构假三层法国民居建筑。法国建筑讲究点缀在自然中，并不在乎占地面积的大小，追求色彩和内在联系，让人感到有很大的活动空间。法式建筑风格还有一个特点是建筑整体方面有着严格的把握，善于在细节雕琢上下工夫，并且十分推崇优雅、高贵和浪漫，这是一种基于对理想情境的考虑，追求建筑的诗意、诗境，力求在气韵上给人深度的感染。法式建筑是经典的，不是时尚的。

Villa Six in Xing Guo Hotel is a three-storied French-style residence of brick and timber. In the French architectural style, houses are set in nature, emphasizing the color and the inner connection more than the size to create the feeling of being spacious. Another trait of the French building is the strict standard about the building as a whole and expert in working on the details. The French architecture, worshipping elegance noble and romance, takes into account of ideal. It tries to impress man with the poetic sentiment it strives to create. The French building is more in keeping with a classical style rather than being fashionable.

六号楼始建于1922年，当时的建筑面积约为250平方米。1935年扩建东南部分后，建筑面积达到620平方米。这座法式别墅还是一个新与旧完美结合的建筑典范，可以明显看出加建的建筑，但新的建筑与旧建筑并没有冲突和抵触，甚至还有些互补和相得益彰的感觉。

With the construction started in 1922, Villa Six had a floor area of 250 square meters. The expansion of the southeast part in 1935 added the area to 620 square meters. So this French-style villa is a perfect example of the combination of the old and the new. The old and the new, which is quite conspicuous, complement and perfect each other instead of conflicting and colliding.

四坡屋面，铺灰色板瓦，舒展、简练的屋顶造型，在不同季节的阳光下会衍生出不同的梦境般的浪漫。南侧屋面上开设一长条形天窗用于屋顶层的采光及通风。该建筑平面设计自由，不拘一格，东侧设二层圆形阳光室，使得整个生活空间在浪漫的基础上获得了一种居住的乐趣，令人体味到对法式

❧六号楼
side entrance of Villa Six

建筑精髓的承袭。西端有一层圆形起居室，二层为露天平台，混凝土宝瓶栏杆。主建筑二层朝南开设大面积玻璃窗，屋面做成跌坡形，形成强烈的视觉对比，山墙檐口曲折，层次丰富。

The hip roof, the grey tiles and the concise roof design create different dream-like romance in different seasons. On the south roof there is a rectangle skylight for the lighting and ventilation of the top floor. Designed freely, the building has a two-storied solaria on the east, making life in it great fun on the basis of romance. The design expresses an inheritance of the essence of French architecture. On the west side is a circular sitting-room on the first floor and a terrace on the second floor with the concrete vase railing. The large-sized glass window facing south on the second floor of the main building and the slope-shaped roof create strong visual contrast.

❧六号楼侧面
a flank of Villa Six

一段有趣的商战故事
A Story of Commercial Competition

据说，六号楼曾经的一任主人，便是当时上海滩著名的美商海宁洋行（他们接手了部分太古洋行所拥有的住宅，包括一号楼）。而这海宁洋行，后来居然和我国食品工业的著名品牌——上海益民食品一厂发生过一些有趣的商战故事。

It is said that Villa Six was home to Henningsen Produce Company, a well-known American company in old Shanghai. It was this very firm that later became involved in an interesting commercial competition with Shanghai Yi Min No.1 Foods （Group） Co., Ltd., a famous brand in the nations national food industry.

可能有人不知道上海益民食品一厂（以下简称：

益民一厂），但江、浙、沪一带上了年纪的老人家，大凡不会有人不知道“美女牌”棒冰、“美女牌”冰淇淋……产品类别之多，品种之全，让人目不暇接，尤其是上海人，大概都吃过该厂生产的冰淇淋和糖果。

❧六号楼内部
the interior of Villa Six

Some people may not know Shanghai Yi Min No.1 Foods（Group）Co.,Ltd.（abbreviated as Yi Min No.1 Factory）. But as for the aged in Jiangsu, Zhejiang and Shanghai, few do not know the products of the factory, such as Hazelwood ice bar and Hazelwood ice cream and a number of other varieties of ice products. Majority of people in Shanghai were consumers of the ice-cream and sweet produced by the factory.

“……在沪首创冷饮的美商海宁洋行，数十年来，一直是冷饮市场的魁首。‘美女牌’棒冰、冰淇淋、紫雪糕，风行全沪，并普及宁沪线一带，当年声威之盛，无出其右。在一九三四年，全年营业额，据该洋行高级职员说，达到七十万美金。头一次的‘凡而佛’牌纸包冰淇淋，竟是远涉重洋，从美国带到上海，更衬托出一种‘名贵’之味道。……目前每日冷饮销路，以棒冰为例总数在三万打至四万打左右，在天气大热时，曾销到四万打，掌握最高销售纪录……”

“Henningsen Produce Company, first engaged in ice cream in Shanghai, was unsurpassed for a dozen of years or more. Hazelwood ice cream bar, ice cream choice was once well-known not only in Shanghai but in Nan Jing and the areas between Shanghai and Nan Jing. The yearly revenue of 1934, according to a senior employee, was as much as 700,000 dollars. The very first ice cream, coming from America to Shanghai, for the present, the daily sale, with the ice bar as an example, is between 30,000 to 40,000 dozen."

益民食品一厂的前身，乃是由美商海宁生于1913年在虹口区沙泾港路250号创建的美商美发公司，是一家蛋品加工厂。民国十三年改为海宁洋行，1927年海宁生开始用机械方法生产棒冰，成了我国最早的冷饮厂家。当时产品为圆柱形，日产量只有2,000 ~ 3,000根。1932年该厂把棒冰模具改为扁长形，棒冰品种除果味外，还生产赤豆、绿豆棒冰、2,000克马口铁听装冰淇淋、320克三色和香草大冰砖及双色纸杯、紫雪糕等。1941年12月，太平洋战争爆发，美商海宁洋行由日本明治产业株式会社接管，1945年8月，抗日战争胜利，被日军接管的海宁洋行随后由国民党政府还给美商。

The predecessor of Yi Min No.1 Factory was an egg processing plant founded by Henningsen in 1931 at 250, Sha Jinggang Road, Hong Kou district. In 1927, Henningsen started to use machines in the production of ice cream, becoming the earliest ice cream manufacturer in China. When the Pacific War broke out in December, 1941, Henningsen Produce Company was taken over by Meji industrial Co.Ltd. The victory of the Anti-Japanese War in August 1945 saw the return of the company through the Kuomintang Government.

当时的海宁洋行为了推销冷饮，定制了大批柜台式大型冰箱，分发给各经销点。冰箱正面黄色，有蓝色英文海宁洋行字样。冰箱供经销点免费使用，只需负担电费。海宁洋行有专用冷藏送货汽车，在市内依照一定路线运行，按经销点需要送货上门。由于海宁洋行的产品都是直接供应零售点，不经过批发商中间环节，虽然本身没有门店，实际上所有经销点都是它的门店。而大规模的机械化生产，既保证了质量，又降低了成本。

To promote the products, Henningsen Produce Company made by order a large batch of refrigerators and distributed them to the sales shops. The front side was yellow with the English name of Henningsen in blue. With the refrigerators free,

六号楼楼梯 the staircase in the Villa Six

the sales shops only needed to pay the bill of electricity. Henningsen Produce Company had special vans made for the delivery of ice cream and sent the needed products to their sales shops on regular routes. With the Henningsen Produce Company supplying the retailers directly, the wholesaler was just omitted. Though Henningsen Produce Company had no shops of its own, in some way, all the retailers were its shops. The mechanized mass-production guaranteed the quality while reducing the cost.

1948年，海宁洋行被国民党收购，改为第一粮秣厂，但第一粮秣厂收购的只是海宁洋行的设备，未收购“美女牌”冰淇淋配方技术。美商海宁生到杨树浦另寻场地，与英商怡和蛋厂合资开设海和有限公司，继续生产冰淇淋，注册商标为“美女牌”，是新中国成立前我国最大的冷饮厂，产量占全国的70%。

新中国成立后，第一粮秣厂被接收，1950年，成立益民工业公司，益民食品一厂不愿放弃冷饮这个市民夏天消暑的食品，又开始了冷饮的恢复生产。“光明牌”冰淇淋生产出来了，但销售情况不好。市民不认“光明牌”冰淇淋，还是喜欢吃“美女牌”冰淇淋。为了让“光明牌”把“美女

牌”比下去，除了口感上要超过它，还要有大手笔，把广告变活，要让印在包装纸上的“光明”变成家喻户晓的名牌。为此，厂里成立宣传组，首先，负责供销业务的徐永强与上海所有的电台都联系好，在同一时间，所有电台都广播“光明牌”冰淇淋广告；他们与上海所有报纸的广告版也都联系好，同时刊登“光明牌”广告；上海各个交通要道都有“光明牌”的广告。除此之外，他们还组织宣传队上街宣传。把一辆美国生产的旧汽车改装成宣传车，车头上“光明问世”四个大字，围绕着火炬形的“光明牌”商标引人注目。这样一支浩浩荡荡的宣传队伍，第一次出来，到了嘉兴路桥就被交通警察拦住了，以影响交通为由，不准通行。同志们自有办法，一方面向交通警察说明“光明牌”和“美女牌”竞赛的意义，另一方面又找军管会进行疏通，以后再出去宣传，交通警察不但不阻拦，还主动在前面开道，维持秩序。

The vast promotion team, on its very first round, was stopped at Jia Xing Bridge by the police for it held up the traffic. The team did not give up. They tried to explain to the police the significance of the contest and sought help from the Military Council. From then on, whenever they took to the street, the police, instead of stopping, volunteered to maintain order for the promotion.

今天，当我们打开那变黄变脆的报纸，从“光明牌”的广告及记者写的报道中，仍然可以感受到当年商战的激烈，如同置身于那场争夺市场的酣战之中。

Today when you unfold the old newspaper and read the reports and the advertisements of the Bright, you can still be hallucinated and feel yourself present in that fierce competition.

六号楼二层露台
terrace on the second floor

七号楼（迴峰楼）：依稀可见昔日的辉煌

Villa Seven: Past Glory

兴国路78号

78, Xing Guo Road

2003年公布为长宁区登记不可移动文物

Proclaimed as the Registered Immovable Cultural Relics of Chang Ning District in 2003.

七号楼全景图

a panoramic view of Villa Seven

❧天花吊灯
the ceiling pendant lamp

如果你认为陆家嘴、淮海路商业街、新天地、外滩等上海高档地段应该是全中国地皮最贵的地方，那就错了；只有当你亲自走过湖南路、武康路、兴国路、泰安路之后，你才会发觉，其实居住也可以成为艺术，并且是谱写着上海百年历史中中最为奢华的生活艺术。

You are easily misled to believe that the houses situated in Lu Jiazui, the commercial district on Huai Hai Road, Xin Tian Di, and the Bund should be the most expensive in China. Only when you have been to Hu Nan Road, Wu Kang Road, Xing Guo Road and Tai'an Road can you realize that living is also an art and actually the most luxurious living art in the recent one hundred years of history of Shanghai.

兴国路向来是万顷繁华地，沿线辐射出的许多小路，无一不盛开在梧桐树的脉络里，移步皆是民国旧景象——独栋洋楼、别墅酒店、欧式公寓，大多在门牌号下附着铭牌，介绍其来龙去脉。信手拈来便可见各色外商使节、民国政要、名流权贵的名字。听起来这样煊赫而咄咄逼人，但在午后极长的日光下，梧桐树间寂然无声，只觉得亲切而平和。

Xing Guo Road, the axis of boom of all the time, and the surrounding paths are all in the shade of plane trees. Everything in sight says of the the mansions, the villa hotels, and the European-style apartments, whose nameplates explain the history of the building. A causal look might bring in sight the names of a variety of celebrities, an ambassador, a politician or a dignitary. It all sounds illustrious and impressive. Yet in the afternoon sunshine and the tranquil shade, all these become friendly and approachable.

兴国宾馆内的七号楼建于20世纪30年代，建筑面积为952平方米。这是一座融入自然环境、充满诗情画意的英式花园别墅，使人仿若置身动画般的仙境美景。表面上看这座建筑用材似乎并不特别，但在造型、线条方面却独具一格、别出心裁，像是用简单普通的布料剪裁和缝制出精美雅致的服装一般，是一个自然与建筑和谐统一结合的典范。

Built in the 1930s, Villa Seven was an English-style garden villa. It is so blended with nature that it makes one feel in the wonderland. The building materials seemed pretty common, yet the shape and the lines are quite unique. It is a classic example of the perfect combination of nature and architecture, just like an exquisite costume made out of ordinary cloth.

英国历史源远流长，英式花园别墅也体现出一种完全不同的生活理念。英国人的信条是“工作是为更好地享受生活，但生存不仅是为了工作”，因此，英国人特别懂得享受生活，英国人也特别懂得心情舒畅地享受阳光。可以说，英国人理想中的美丽风景和别墅是这样的：房前是绿色草坪，屋后是郁郁葱葱的树林。因此英式别墅也凝结着英国建筑的精华。表面富丽堂皇，又不缺乏文化和艺术品位。

With the long rich history of Britian, the English-style garden villa reflects a totally different concept of life. The Englishmen believe in working for life, instead of living for working. As a result, they know how to enjoy life and sunshine. The ideal villa of the English is like this: a lawn in front and the dense woods at the back. So the English-style villa reflects the essence of English architecture, magnificent and abundant in cultural and artistic taste.

英式别墅的屋顶造型多姿多彩，不论是几百年历史的老房子，还是新建的别墅，都特别注重屋顶的造型，而且同样采用砖瓦和木头的栋梁结构，其传统的建筑艺术、工艺和方法得到了很好保留。七号楼也是砖木结构假三层。南面底层有突出的多边形门厅，上为二层平台，设混凝土镂花栏杆，南面底层均为落地长窗。陡坡红瓦屋面，三面山墙开三扇老虎窗面。两座红砖清水烟囱穿出屋面，烟囱口有英国建筑特有的多边曲折装饰。外墙水泥砂浆刷面，山墙部分干粘小河卵石。

The British villa, whether it is a hundred-year-old building or a newly-built one, always gives priority to the design of the roofs, which, though diversified, are always of timber and tiles. The traditional art, craft and methods are preserved pretty well. Villa Seven is a three-storied house of brick and timber structure. On the ground floor in the south is a protruding polygon lobby, above which is a terrace with concrete railing. There are French windows on the southern side of the ground floor. The slope roof is of the red tiles with three dormer windows on the three gables. Two red brick chimneys stand out over the roof with uniquely English polygonal decorations at their gutters. The exterior wall is brushed with cement mortar, and the gable walls with cobblestones.

英资德和洋行创始人

The Founder of Lester, Johnson & Morriss

这座七号楼也是当年叱咤上海滩的英商德和洋行给这座城市留下的建筑遗产。1917年建成的南京路上的先施公司、1924年兴建的中山东一路16号台湾银行办公大楼（现在为招商银行大楼）、1921年兴建的中山东一路5号日清大楼（现在为华夏银行上海分行）……都是由德和洋行设计的。最近，七号楼的新一任租方在老房子里发现了当年德和洋行的设计图稿。

Villa Seven is a heritage building designed by the Architects Lester, Johnson & Morriss. The firm designed a number of other buildings in Shanghai, the Sincere & Co. Ltd. built in 1917 on Nan Jing Road, the Bank of Taiwan Building at 16 Zhong Shan Road built in 1924 which is now the China Merchant Bank Building, and the Nissin Shipping Building built in 1921, now the Hua Xia Bank, Shanghai Branch. A recent tenant of Villa Seven found the original blueprints in the house.

德和洋行的创始人亨利·雷士德，在上海开埠后的历史长河中可算是一个富有传奇色彩的外国人。他1839年出生在英国，在英国获得建筑学学士学位后于1867年来到上海，成为最早进入上海的建筑师之一。他到上海的当年就与租界工部局签订了一份3年的服务合同，负责租界的城市规划和建设监督。雷士德以他测绘技术的专长，协助法租界公董局绘制出版了上海法租界的第一幅地图。

The founder of Lester，Johnson & Morriss was Henry Lester, a legendary foreigner in Shanghai. Born in 1839 in Britain, he came to Shanghai after he had received his Bachelor of Architecture degree in 1867, becoming one of the earliest foreign architects in the city. When he arrived in Shanghai he made contact with the Shanghai Municipal Council in charge for the city planning of the foreign settlements. With his background in topography, he helped the administration of the Concession, in publishing the first map of the French Concession of Shanghai.

当时，一位叫史密士的美国人创建的史密士洋行已购进了租界的大量土地，成为上海早期最大的地产商之一，但房地产的开发和建设必须有专业的建筑师，于是，应史密士之邀，雷士德就成了史密士的合作伙伴和洋行的主要股东之一。当19世纪80年代史密士退休后，史密士洋行名下的房地产几乎全部落在雷士德的名下。在20世纪二三十年代的地产界，雷士德成为仅次于哈同而超过沙逊的房地产巨子。

七号楼的彩色玻璃窗
a stained glass window in Villa Seven

At that time an American named Smith, established a

Shanghai Real Estate Agency who bought a substantial amount of land and became one of the largest land agents in Shanghai. Yet real estate needed professional architects. Therefore, Lester, at the invitation of Smith, became the partner and major shareholder of the firm. At the moment of Smith's retirement to America, Lester became the owner of almost all of the property of the firm. In the 1920s and 1930s, he possessed more estates on Nan Jing Road, than Sasson and was second only to Hardoon, becoming the illustrious giant in real estate of Shanghai.

当雷士德与工部局的3年合同期满后，他即创办了德和洋行，专营建筑设计、土木工程、测绘检验、房地产抵押贷款，数额巨大。以后，他的英国同胞马立斯、约翰逊等人入股，德和洋行遂成为当年上海实力最强的建筑设计事务所之一。在以后的几十年时间里，雷士德在上海留下了不少英国式的建筑，如今尚在的主要作品除了上述那些，还包括普益大楼；仁济医

七号楼附近的树丛
the thicket around Villa Seven

院；《字林西报》大楼；雷士德医、工学院；迦陵大楼；三菱银行；兴国宾馆七号楼……

When his three year contract came to an end, Lester founded an agency specialized in architectural designing, engineering, surveying and mortgage. Later on, the partnership of his compatriots, Johnson and Morriss, rendered the firm the most powerful architecture design company in Shanghai. In the following decades, Lester left behind quite a few English-style buildings. Besides those mentioned above, there are others, such as Asia Realty Co. Building, Yan Chai Hospital, the North China Daily News Building, Henry Lester Institute of Technical Education, Hamilton House, Mitsubishi Bank and Villa Seven of Xing Guo Hotel.

雷士德还通过以房地产参股合资或收购股票的方式，成为上海多家商行、公司的股东或主要股东。他还是旧中国外资在华的最大报业印刷出版集团——字林洋行的董事长以及英商上海电车公司的大股东和董事会成员。

Through stock acquisition or joint venture, Lester became the shareholder of many firms in Shanghai. He was also the president of Pickwoad and Co, the largest newspaper publisher in China, and the major shareholder and board member of Shanghai Electric Construction Co. Ltd.

雷士德的私生活极其严肃，且自奉节俭。传说他的三个哥哥相继病逝后，医生叮嘱他，婚姻会直接影响他的健康，甚至生命。他虽在上海拥有大量房地产，却长年住在英侨总会的陈年老屋里，没有自备汽车和黄包车，外出大多乘电车，平时所穿衣服、所戴领带多是朋友用过的旧货。

Lester was very solemn and frugal in life. It is said that after the successive deaths of his three brothers, the doctor told him that marriage would threaten his health, he lived permanently in an old house belonging to the Association of English. He did not have his own car or rickshaw and his clothes or ties were all second-hand ones from his friends.

这个英国人于1867年来到上海后，从此再没离开，1926年5月他在上海去世，下葬于外国坟山即今静安公园内，最终长眠在了这片异国的土地上。令人感动的是，在一个世纪前，这位来自英伦的外国人，终身未娶的他，身后留下了1,430余万两银子的巨额遗产，由于其大多为房地产，仅土地就有六百余亩（400,000平方米），到第二年重新估价时，总值就已达到2,000万两银子，而当时汇丰银行上海分行的注册资本也不过2,000万两，可见其生前实力之雄厚。

Since his arrival in Shanghai, he never once left the city from the day he arrived. He died in Shanghai in May 1926, and was buried in Foreign Cemetery （today's Jing'an Park）, staying forever in this land. It is moving that this foreigner had been an embodiment of internationalism a century ago. He never married, he left behind a legacy of some 14.30 million tael of silver. Most of his heritage was in real estate, with land as much as 400,000 square meters. The new assessment in the following year made the total value of the land ascended to 20 million tael of silver. And the registered capital of the Shanghai Branch of Hong Kong and Shanghai Banking Corporation was about 20 million then.

根据其遗嘱，在上海创建了以他名字命名的基金会，造福于中国人。基金会成员由工部局指派的人员和雷士德生前指定的亲朋好友组成，遗嘱上写着，“在将近60年中，我主要的和永久的定居地一直在中国上海，现在如此，今后也将如此”。他将财产分配给圣路加、仁济、同仁等医院及盲人院和开办教育事业。他知道黄包车车夫的辛苦，将5万两银子捐给“上海车夫福音会”。因此也有人把他称为“来自英伦的大慈善家”。

According to his will, a trust was to be established in his name for the well-being of Chinese and the members of the trust were made up of the staff nominated by the Municipal Council and the relatives and friends of Lester's. The will reads, “for almost 60 years I have lived, and will live permanently in Shanghai, China.” He allotted his money to St. Luke's hospital, Yan Chai Hospital, Tong Ren Hospital and Hospital for the Blind, where he contributed to the education. He knew the hardship of the rickshaw puller and donated 50,000 tael of silver to an organization for the rickshaw men of Shanghai. Therefore he was referred to as the philanthropist from Britain.

雷士德把上海视为自己的家乡，希望上海发展强大，他在遗嘱中明确说明要在上海建立一所医工学院。1927年5月，雷士德基金会按照他的遗嘱筹建医药研究所和工学院。雷士德医药研究所在1932年11月先行落成。

七号楼的红砖烟囱 the redbrick chimney of Villa Seven

次年，雷士德医学院开学，规定以华人子弟为主要学生，并适当接纳除英、美、法三国以外的其他国籍学生。

Lester regarded Shanghai as his hometown, and wished it to be prosperous. In his will he made it clear that a medical and technological institute should be built. In May, 1927, the Henry Lester Trust, according to his will, embarked upon the founding of an institute of medical research and an institute of technology. In November, 1932, Henry Lester Institute of Medical Research was completed. In the following year, Henry Lester Institute for Medical Research was opened. It mainly enrolled Chinese students and occasionally some students from nations other than Britain, America and France.

用雷士德基金建造的雷士德医学院和雷士德工学院如今已成为上海市优秀近代保护建筑。

Henry Lester Institute for Medical Research and Henry Lester Institute of Technical Education founded by Henry Lester Trust is listed as an Outstanding Historical Building of Shanghai.

颜料大王周宗良后人的住宅

The Residence of the Descendants of Zhou Zongliang, the King of Pigment

七号楼曾经的主人，则是上海滩赫赫有名的德商洋行买办、颜料大王周宗良（1875—1957）的后人住宅。

Villa Seven was once the residence of the descendants of Zhou Zongliang, the famous comprador for German companies and the King of Pigment.

周宗良先后任多家德商洋行买办长达35年，为德国公司操纵中国市场染料，由此成了国内可数的富豪之一。

Zhou Zongliang served as the comprador of several German firms for as long as 35 years, and contributed to the manipulation of German pigment in Chinese market, becoming one of the few millionaires at home.

周宗良，清光绪元年（1875年）出生在浙江宁波。其父是牧师，并在当地主营规模不小的油漆店，小有资产。周宗良幼年就读于宁波耶稣教会的

七号楼的楼梯
the staircase in Villa Seven

斐迪中学，离校后进入宁波海关工作。他勤奋好学，业余向洋税务司夫人学习英语，不过数年英语口语就相当流利。之后脱离海关转入德商爱礼司洋行在宁波的经销行美益颜料店工作。此时德国谦信洋行大班轧罗门到宁波调查销售情况，当地颜料号经理大都不懂外语，遂请周宗良任译员。轧罗门在宁波逗留数天，对周宗良的殷勤接待和敏捷才华颇为赏识。不久，周脱离美益号，于光绪三十一年来上海另谋出路，在谦信洋行任跑楼。当时在中国经营染料业务的洋行有禅臣、元亨、天福、谦信、裕兴、爱礼司等十几家，竞争十分激烈。周宗良以其英语和社交上的优势，得到谦信洋行老板的赏识，很快就取代了该行原先的买办姜炳生，坐上了买办交椅。那时华人当买办需以道契作担保，周氏其时立足尚未稳，未置办房地产，就由他的伙伴、后来亦成为颜料巨商的苏州人、瑞康颜料号的经理贝润生借出道契。

❧七号楼的彩色玻璃窗
a stained glass window in Villa Seven

Zhou Zongliang was born in Ningbo in the year 1875. His father, running a large-paint shop, was also a clergyman. After graduating from middle school, Zhou Zongliang worked for the Customs office of Ningbo. He was very eager to learn and in his spare time he learned English from the wife of the foreign commissioner. Years later he was quite fluent in English. Shortly he left the employ of the Customs house and worked in a pigment shop established

七号楼的彩色玻璃窗
stained glass windows in Villa Seven

by Alice Co. At that time a German Taipan conducted a survey in Ningbo. Almost none of the managers in the pigment shops understood a foreign language; Zhou Zongliang was invited to be the interpreter. During the Taipan's stay in Ningbo, Zhou's hospitality and talents was appreciated. Soon Zhou Zongliang left the pigment shop and came to Shanghai to serve as the translator in Schlesinger. In China then there were a dozen of foreign firms engaged in the pigment and the competition was very fierce. Zhou Zongliang, with his advantage of English and his demenaour, gained favor from the Taipan of Schlesinger and pretty soon replaced the former comprador Jiang Bingsheng. At that time land lease contract was needed as a guarantee if a Chinese national wanted to be a comprador. With his just coming to Shanghai and having no estate, Zhou Zongliang borrowed a contract from his partner, Bei Runsheng, who came from Suzhou and later on also became the pigment tycoon.

1914年第一次世界大战爆发，在华经商的德国人纷纷打包回国。当时的谦信洋行已是在华最大的德国洋行，不仅在沪置有大量房地产，而且贮存的染料也数量巨大。该行老板轧罗门深恐大战中谦信遭受损失，就与周宗良密商，将谦信在沪的不动产的户名全部改为周宗良，托其隐匿保管；而谦信所有的染料，全部折价，以很低的价格卖给周氏，周氏接受了这一计划。不久，战争期间亚欧之间运输断绝，进口染料由于货源断绝一下子成了紧俏商品，而周宗良手里掌握了全部谦信的仓储，因而一跃成为颜料业的巨擘，成了沪上数得着的大富豪。

Due to World War I, many German businessmen left Shanghai. Schlesinger one of the largest German companies in China, not only possessed a number of estates in Shanghai, but had a considerable storage of pigment. Afraid of the possible damage from the war, the Taipan transferred all the estates in Shanghai under the name of Zhou Zongliang, and sold all the pigment in the firm to Zhou at an incredibly low price. With the transportation links between Europe and Asia cut off, the imported pigment, because of the shortage, became a difficult commodity and Zhou Zongliang, in possession of all the storage of Schlesinger, became the pigment giant and millionaire in Shanghai overnight.

1924年，德国一些主要染料化工厂为了加强与其他资本主义国家企业的竞争能力，防止在互相竞争中削弱实力，实行了行业大联合，组织了一个托拉斯集团，名为大德染料公司，统一管理各厂家的对外销售业务。与此相对应，就在上海联合成立了一个德孚洋行，作为中国独家经理行，把原先在沪的德商企业，包括谦信、爱礼司、裕兴、禅臣、礼和、拜耳、广丰等洋行中的染料业务，统统划归德孚集中经营。德孚共有5个买办，分别挂牌“爱礼司买办间”、“裕兴买办间”等，而总买办一职又落到了周宗良头上，他就成了德国染料在华的总推销人。周宗良为德孚先后在武汉、长沙、济南、青岛、天津、重庆等大城市开设了分行，又竭力为他主持的谦和号在各地发展销售点，从原来的几十个分支号迅速发展到全国二百多个销售点，资本也从原来的140万银两增加到400万银两。1927年后他任中国银行董事、中央银行理事和国民政府公债基金保管委员会委员，并投资电气、轮船、纺织等实业。1930年又独资设立周宗记商号，经销拜耳西药、谦信洋行制作的汽油灯、洋杂货和颜料等，并经营房地产和其他投资。此外，又与贝润生合资开设恒孚钱庄。

In 1924, the major German Dye chemical plants formed a trust as an industrial combination in China, named Pan-German Dye Company, to become more competitive that other capitalistic stale enterprices, and prevent them from being weakened in the competitiom. The dye business German firms in Shanghai were united under Farben. The company had five comprador, called Alice Comprador Shop an Xing Comprador Shop with Zhou as the general comprador and the top salesmen of German dye in Shanghai. Zhou Zongliang opened factories one after another for the company in such major cities as Wuhan, Changsha, Jinan, Qingdao, Tianjin and Chungking and strained hard to deve retailers, increasing the shops from dozen to more than two hundred and the income to 4 million tael of silver. In 1927, he became the director of Bank of China, a member of Central Bank, Board of Trustees of the Bond Funds. He made a number of investments in electricity, shipping and textiles. In 1930 he founded independently his own shop dealing in gasoline burners produced by Schlesinger, medicines produced by Bayer, imported groceries and dyes. He was also involved in real estate and co-founded Heng Fu

Money House.

俗话说“树大招风”，周宗良生意做得大了，对他关注的人也就越来越多，最后终于被日伪时期上海魔窟“76号”的行动队队长吴世宝“相中”，派了一帮人一大早冲进其前院，借口周与重庆银行界有来往，要把他绑票。周宗良早就听说外边风声不好，请了几个保镖日夜守护，每天早晨去德孚洋行上班时，先派人在门口察看动静，没有可疑迹象才肯出门。可是绑匪那天已不等他出门，直接冲了进来，周宗良见势不好，急忙从后门逃走，跑到隔壁法租界巡捕房寻求保护。绑匪找不到周宗良，结果把他的太太绑走，最后花了4万元“运动费”，才把人赎了出来。

As the old saying goes, a great tree inspires the wind. With the expansion of his business, Zhou Zongliang caught more and more attention and finally got the notice from Wu Shibao, who was the leader of the action team of No.76, a den during the puppet period. Wu sent a group of bandits rushed into Zhou's front yard and intended to kidnap him with the excuse that he had connections with the banks in Chungking. In fact, Zhou had learned the bad circumstances and hired some bodyguards defending him day and night. He wouldn't walk out to his office without his guards watching out every morning. However, the bandits rushed into before he went out on that morning. Zhou ventured out from back door and made his way to the neighboring French Concession and sought protection from the police station there. Having not found Zhou, the bandits kidnapped his wife instead and let her free only after they got 40,000 Yuan.

抗战胜利后，国民党回来接收上海，为了振兴经济，也动脑“请财神”了。当时吴国桢当市长，客客气气地摆了数桌酒宴，把上海滩的工商巨子都请了去，而排在首席的则是周宗良。当酒过三巡，吴国桢亮出真牌，请大家为市政府捐款，周宗良提笔写了50万元。

After the victory of the Anti-Japanese War, the Kuomintang took over Shanghai. To boost the economy, it thought about the "mammon". The mayor prepared a feast and the industrial and commercial giants in Shanghai were invited along Zhou Zongliang on the top. During the banquet, the mayor made his intention known, namely, he wanted them to donate for the Municipal Government. Zhou

Zongliang picked up a pen and wrote down 500,000 Yuan.

此外，对于造医院，周宗良似乎格外热情。他曾捐给德国人办的宝隆医院一笔较大的款子，在抗战前还曾与同济大学商定，投资100万元建造一所宗良医院，协议已经鉴定，后因“八一三”战起，计划未能实现。抗战初期，他还在江宁路开办了一所伤兵医院，成为中国红十字会的创办人之一。1948年6月，周宗良定居香港，1957年病逝。

In addition, Zhou seemed especially passionate about building hospitals. He donated a large amount of money to the German founded Paulun Hospital and he reached an agreement with Tong Ji University to build Zong Liang Hospital. The contract was already signed before the plan was miscarried by the war after the August 13 Incident. In the first phase of Anti-Japanese war, he started a hospital for the wounded soldiers on Jiang Ning Road and became one of the founders of the Red Cross Society of China. He went to Hongkong in June 1948 and passed away in 1957.

周宗良的后代中有一个孙子叫周裕农，在国内外经济界很有影响，他毕业于美国加州大学伯克利分校，获电脑软件学学士和工商管理硕士学位，专修财务，曾任美国芝加哥国民银行的经理和美国休斯敦银行香港分行的买办，自1980年起是香港中华总商会会董。他曾担任中国银行总行代表，主导成立中国在海外的第一家国际合资公司CCIC。他的外公周均时曾任同济大学第十二任校长，与朱家骅为留德同学，后来不幸被蒋介石杀害。正是周裕农这一房，曾住在兴国宾馆七号楼。

Among his descendants, there was a grandson named Zhou Yunnong who was very influential in economics both at home and abroad. Having graduated from University of California in Berkeley with a Bachelor's degree in computer science and a MBA, he served as the manager of First Chicago Corporation and the comprador of Bank of Houston in Hong Kong. Since 1980 he was the chairman of China General Chamber of Commerce in Hong Kong. While serving as the representative of the Bank of China, he organized China's first overseas joint venture CCIC. His maternal grandfather Zhou Junshi, the 12th president of Tongji University, was the classmate of Zhu Jiahua when they were in Germany who was unfortunately killed later by Chiang Kai-Shek.

绮石楼：见证上海过去的流金岁月

Qi Shi: Witness the Old Days in Shanghai

兴国路78号

78, Xing Guo Road

绮石楼侧面
side of Qi Shi

有人说，“城市是有生命的，老建筑就是城市的记忆”。兴国宾馆，在这一海派文化荟萃之地，20世纪三四十年代，众多的名人和商业巨子聚集于此，也形成了上海最具特色的老洋房住宅群落，这些历史建筑，其中有不少是半个多世纪前的经典，这是历史留给上海的珍贵遗产。

Someone once said that a city is living and the old buildings are the memory of a city. With the Xing Guo Hotel, the vibrant center of the Shanghai culture attracted a number of celebrities and businessmen in 1930s and 1940s, hence the most unique group of villas. Many of these villas, classics for more than half a century, were a precious heritage and history is left for Shanghai.

一座有着美丽名字的别墅
The Villa with a Beautiful Name

老洋房是上海最经典的住宅，这些充满异国情调的花园别墅大多有着显赫一时的背景，或是诗情画意的浪漫故事，童话般的别墅不仅是当年人人钦羡的地方，现在的年轻人也对这些豪华的建筑有着无限憧憬。

As one of the most classical residences in Shanghai, these exotic garden villas either glorious backgrounds and romance connected with them. These fairy tale-like villas used to be and still are the dreams of many.

绮石楼，就是这样一座有着奇异美丽名称的别墅。

Qi Shi is just such a villa with a beautiful name.

相传这里曾经住着一位德国医学家，因为很欣赏中国明代末期、以善治虚劳病名重一时、著有《理虚元鉴》的医学家汪绮石先生，而将自己的住宅命名为绮石楼。

The legend says that a German medical scientist once lived at the property, and due to his admiration of Wang Qishi, the medical scientist from the Dynasty Ming who was famous for his cure of the consumptive disease and his works *Theory on Original Asthenia*, he named his residence Qi Shi.

汪绮石先生开创论治虚劳“三本”、“二统”学说，对后世治疗虚损性疾病颇有启迪，他的生平履历已经无从考证，但这栋和他同名的上海老洋

绿树掩映中的绮石楼
Qi Shi set off with the green

❧远眺绮石楼
Qi Shi seen from a distance

房，却历经风雨，见证着上海过去的流金岁月。

Wang Qi Shi created a number of new theories regarding a cure for consumptive disease, which are still influential to no less a degree to this day. His life story is untraceable, yet the building of his namesake bears testimony to the past glory of Shanghai.

兴国宾馆静，而且静得美，那里绿树参天，各式各样的洋房建筑在夜幕中显露着异国他乡的风姿，而

偶尔从哪栋房里传来的飘逸在晚空中的小提琴声和钢琴声，在夜晚的轻风中为人们描绘着没有边际的幻影，把人们引入奇思妙想中。

The quietness in Xing Guo Hotel is app-ealing. The trees, the diversified exotic villas and the occasional violin or piano sounds make the imagination roam far and wide, taking people into the dreamland.

在兴国宾馆影影绰绰的绿意中，绮石楼的门牌并不十分显眼，这栋四百多平方米的老洋房精致地藏匿于一条几乎被绿树淹没的路上。如今，它再一次被赋予新的生命，似乎在寻求某种方式，把经过岁月沉淀的美绽放在这个时代中。

The doorplate of Qi Shi is not very obvious, this old Villa, with 400 square meters, is perfectly hidden on a road which is almost totally concealed in the green. Today, it is given a new life. It seems as if it is striving for some means to bring the beauty precipitated through time to the present.

绮石楼，是盛开在上海租界文化土壤深处的一朵浅淡的奇葩。推门走进这座20世纪初的建筑，西式的外观之下有浓郁的东方色彩，在历经岁月积累和会所主人的精心安排后，它以经典、精致和浓浓的上海韵味，展示着自己作为高级会所的诱人魅力。别墅主人不仅让人们想起了记忆中的老上海，更融合了中西合璧的设计理想，精辟诠释上海奢华和新上海摩登。

Qi Shi is a mildly fragrance blossom that is deeply rooted in Shanghai concession culture. If you push open this building of the dawn of last century, you will find that the western appearance harbors rich eastern elements. Precipitated in time and designed extraordinarily by the owner, the club, with a classic and exquisite Shanghai appeal, shows its irresistible charms as a high-level club. The owner not only constructed the memorable old Shanghai he blended the west and the east, a brilliant interpretation about the luxurious and modern Shanghai.

细腻的线条、质朴的色彩都显示出它的落落大方和文化底蕴。环境充满了优雅的贵气，在这个很“老上海”的地方，每一个设计都独具匠心，每一个角落都是一道风景。

The delicate lines and the simple color talk about its generosity and culture, full of grace and nobility. In this place most reminiscent of old Shanghai, every design is of ingenuity and every corner a sight.

慵懒的下午茶时光
Leisurely Afternoon Tea

一桌一椅、一几一柜，浓郁的东方装修风格，所有的家具都犹如一件件精美的艺术品陈列其中，每一件摆设、每一幅画和每一株花卉都诉说着同一段精美绝伦、古老而又新鲜的故事。身处如此的环境里，什么都变得舒缓下来，矜持起来，旧时的繁华和时过境迁的沉着安静，每个人都怀揣着各自的美妙心情……

The club is typical of the Asian decoration. Every piece furniture, be it a chair, a table, or a cupboard, is like a works of art on display. Every ornament, every painting and every flower tells a beautiful and old story. Present in this surrounding, you will find all slow down and get lost in this hard worn tranquility.

在这样的氛围中，你走到了院子前面，看到了既可以喝咖啡也可以品香茗的桌椅，也看到了草地上的花花树树。英国电影教给我们的温馨下午茶会就在这样的场景中逼真地再现出来。这里的一草一木均渗透着古今，东西各异的文化气质，彼此结合如此完美，仿佛浑然天成的一件令人游目骋怀的艺术品。环境美得让人心醉，到这里来的人，无不深深沉醉于天然优美的花园环境吧。春秋两季在室外闲谈静坐，在阳光下品尝下午茶，一瞬间有时空交错的感觉，更让人感到隐藏不住的贵族气，在上海，曾被遗忘的、奢侈的、浪漫的、神秘的、传说中的东方情调，就在此地复活。

Here in the yard, you cannot fail to see the table and chairs where either coffee or tea is served, and you cannot miss the trees and flowers in the lawn. It is here that is a

❧绮石楼一楼回廊
the terrace on the first floor in Qi Shi

reminder of the cozy afternoon tea which is a familiar scene in English films. It is here that you can feel the difference between the old and the new and that between the West and the East; and it is also here that you feel the perfect combination of all these seemingly conflicting elements. It seems to be a gift from nature that sets the imagination free. Set in this unbelievable beauty, people cannot help being intoxicated. In the autumn and spring, chatting and sipping tea in the afternoon sunshine makes life so beautiful to be true. It is here that the luxurious, romantic and mysterious Eastern complex revives and thrives.

若是有机会到上海，入住兴国宾馆，不妨去一趟绮石楼。有时候，我们的确需要这种醉生梦死的浪漫，去平衡一下在高高写字楼里的压力。

If opportunity arises for you to come to Shanghai and stay in Xing Guo Hotel, do go and see Qi Shi. Occasionally we do need this romance to offset the pressure in the office.

老上海在人们心目中已远远超过对一个年代的回忆而上升为一个理念、一份情怀。梧桐深深，在兴国宾馆，细细品味那一栋栋充满着旧日风情的老洋房，一处处讲述着历史故事的老地方，走进它们，会有一种置身欧陆的感觉。徜徉在这些历史人文丰富的聚集之处，随性抚摩历史的墙壁，走在这些曾有过无数回忆与曾经的老洋房以及老地方中，一切都好像仍在昨日的一个梦里，好似自己也沉浸在旧日的风光里。只是，今日的兴国宾馆，这些历史的遗迹更焕发着不一样的精彩。或许有一天你会发现，消逝的遗迹其实就在你的眼前……

Old Shanghai is more than the memory of an age now, it has become a sentiment. In Xing Guo Hotel, the old villas that tell about the past will bring the illusion of being in Europe. Strolling in this historical place and wandering in these old villas, you might believe this is just a dream of yesterday and you might feel as if you were exactly present in that old age. The Xing Guo Hotel today, however, radiates some different splendor. Maybe one day you will find the fading relic is right there before you.

❧绮石楼一楼内部
the interior on the first floor in Qi Shi

湖南别墅：庭院深深、心事幽幽

Hu Nan Villa: A Villa with an intriguing past

湖南路262号

262, Hu Nan Road

上海市第三批优秀历史建筑

Listed as one of the third batch of Shanghai Outstanding Historical Buildings

从兴国宾馆的另一条路出来，在湖南路转弯，再沿着湖南路往东行，就可以看到一条上海最优雅的小路之一——武康路。这个名字如此耳熟能详，在很多讲到上海的电影和小说里都有这条马路的芳名。

Upon exiting the property and venturing along Xing Guo Road, and turning into Hu Nan Road and walking along you can come to one of the most elegant roads in Shanghai, Wu Kang Road. This name is surely familiar for it appears constantly in films or novels about Shanghai.

浓缩上海百年历史的福开森路

Route Ferguson: A Microcosm of Shanghai in the Early 20th Century

在上海，有64条永不拓宽的马路，其中有一条因其独具魅力而成为上海市政府向全世界重点推出的世博旅游景点之一，这条马路的名字，就叫武康路。这条位于徐汇区北部，北接华山路，南与淮海中路相交的新月形走向的马路，始建于光绪三十三年（1907），至今已有一百多年的历史。据《上海市徐汇区地名志》记载："该路原名福开森路，以美国人福开森姓氏命名。1943年改现名武康路，以浙江省旧县名命名。"

In Shanghai, there are sixty-four roads that are not allowed to be widened, among which is Wu Kang Road, which has become one of the Shanghai tourist attractions for its uniqueness. Located in the north of Xu Hui District, this crescent-shaped road, connecting Hua Shan Road in the north and Middle Huai Hai Road in the South, was first built in 1907, having stood for more than a hundred years. According to Xu Hui District Gazette, this road, originally named after the American Ferguson, was changed to Wu Kang Road in 1943, an old county in Zhejiang province.

在老上海，以外国人人名来命名的马路比比皆是，不足为奇，但是像福开森路这样被人们誉为"浓缩了上海近代百年历史"的名人路，却并不多见，它一度聚集了中国近代一批叱咤风云的人物，如民国第一任总理唐绍仪、文坛巨匠巴金、国母宋庆龄、辛亥革命领导人黄兴，其他的商贾富豪更是无法一一列举。那么，这条马路与福开森又有怎样的缘由呢？这位从美国来的传教士为什么要修这条路呢？

❧湖南别墅的花园
the garden in Hu Nan Villa

In old Shanghai, it was common to see roads that are named after foreigners. Yet Route Ferguson is one of the few, if not the only, to be reputed as the road of celebrities that witnessed the history in the past century.

A number of names that played a role in modern China, such as the first premier in the Republic Tang Shaoyi, The literary giant Ba Jin, the first lady Song Qingling, Huang Xing （the major leader of the Revolution of 1911）, along with countless merchants. What has the road to do with Ferguson, the American missionary?

福开森——这个美利坚合众国的公民，把半个世纪的人生奉献在了中国这块当时还略显贫瘠的土地

上，其在华的传奇历程在今天却知之者甚少。

Ferguson, an American citizen, devoted half a century of his life in China, which was a barren land back then. Yet very few know about him and his legend in Shanghai. Need more background information on him.

在福开森20岁时，也就是1886年，从波士顿大学毕业后就来到了中国，起初在南京任教，很快就出任汇文书院（金陵大学的前身）的校长。清末洋务派大臣盛宣怀受李鸿章之托督办南洋公学（上海交通大学前身），正苦于找不到谙熟现代大学管理的人才，巧遇福开森在上海逗留，遂聘其为“监院”（相当于现在的教务总长）。福开森上任后，为方便师生出行，用自己的薪水修建了这条马路。开始这条路并无确实名称，后法租界在扩大地盘中，与上海宁波同乡会“四明公所”发生冲突，又与英、美、俄等国产生了矛盾。福开森从中调停，最终令各方满意获得解决。

In 1886, at the age of 20, Ferguson graduated from Boston University, and came to China, first as a teacher in Nanjing and then as the president of Nan King University. Sheng Xuanhuai, at the invitation of Li Hongzhang, established Nan Yang College（the predecessor of Shanghai Jiao tong University）. While searching for someone with the background of management, he happened to meet Ferguson who was staying in Shanghai and invited him to be the official principal. Ferguson, for the convenience of the students and faculty, paved the road with his salary. At the beginning, this was a nameless road. Yet later on the French Concession conflicted first with the Clansmen Society of Ningbo and then with Britain, America and Russia in the process of expansion. It was Ferguson who settled the conflicts to the satisfaction of all parties involved.

福开森后来先后加入刘坤一、张之洞幕府，从此涉足中国政治界，还在1910年由于赈灾募集资金有功，被清廷授予二品顶戴，做了中国政府的官。客观地说，福开森为中国的教育、文化事业的发展做了不少贡献。此外，福开森酷爱中国美术和文物，是个中国通，一口流利的中文，让其在中国上层中极受欢迎。

❧湖南别墅的石砌墙柱
the stone wall column of Hu Nan Villa

❧湖南公寓的歇山式屋顶
irimoya roof of Hu NanVilla

Ferguson's successive service in the office of Liu kunyi and that of Zhang Zhidong officially started his political career in China. In 1910 due to his contribution in fund raising, he was granted a mandarin by Chinese government. Honestly speaking, Ferguson contributed considerably to the development of Chinese education and culture. Besides, Ferguson, an ardent lover of Chinese painting and relics, was an old China hand and spoke pretty fluent Chinese, which earned him popularity in the high society.

为了表彰福开森，法租界当局就把他修建的这条马路冠名为福开森路。当时，福开森聘请的教授都住在市区，自从修建了这条马路后教师上班、上学就方便多了，因此，很受师生称赞。福开森路起先是一条土路，两边尽是水稻和菜园及

农舍，河道边池塘密布，散落着许多坟丘。1914年，福开森路正式被划入法租界，法国第一任驻沪领事明梯尼按照当时西方最现代的城市建设理念，实施了武康路沿线的整体规划，并以武康路为中心，将这一规划逐步向周边推进。由于受到来自法兰西科技、资金、文化的强力推动，很快形成了以武康路为标志的法国社区。住在这里的都是西方派驻上海的官员和高级管理人员。

To honor Ferguson, the French named the road he built, Avenue Ferguson. At the time, professor Ferguson invited all who lived in the urban area and the road rendered their way to and back from school much easier. Thus it won praises among students and faculty. At the very beginning, Avenue Ferguson was a muddy road lined with paddy fields, cottages, ponds and even graves. In 1914, Avenue Ferguson was officially included into the French Concession. The first French Consul in Shanghai, in accordance with the modern city construction, implemented the overall planning with Wu Kang road as the center. The French community with Wu Kang Road as a symbol was formed instantly. People that lived here were mostly the Western officials accredited to Shanghai and senior managers.

电影《色·戒》里的最后一段，佳芝叫了辆黄包车，说“去福开森路”。导演把张爱玲原作中的“愚园路”改为“福开森路”，用福开森路取代同样精致华丽的愚园路，可见福开森路在人们心中的地位。

At the very end of the film *Lust, Caution*, Jia Zhi stopped a rickshaw and said, “Go to Avenue Ferguson”. The importance of the Avenue Ferguson can be best

❧湖南别墅的水平红瓦披檐
the horizontal red-tile slope eave

❧乳白色弹涂外墙 the milk-white exterior wall

shown when the director changed Yu Yuan Road in the original work into Avenue Ferguson and substituted Ferguson for the equally luxurious and exquisite Yu Yuan Road.

1941年，太平洋战争爆发，以美国为首的西方与日本交恶，侵华日军占领上海法租界，武康路陷落。1943年，法国宣布放弃以武康路为中心的法租界，汪伪政府乘机宣布“接收”法租界，并将武康路所在法租界改为上海市特别第八区。汪伪政府的“接受”不被国、共两党及国际社会所认可，也不为国内民众所接收。汪精卫因此非常懊恼，却又无计可施，躲在湖南别墅里生闷气。一天，周佛海、胡兰成及汪伪上海市市长等人提出了应对之策，建议汪精卫把“接收”租界的二百多条以外国人命名的马路，全部改成以中国各省、市及部分县级行政区域名称命名，这样做有几大好处：一是显示了汪伪政府的独立、尊严和民族气节，可以摆脱汉奸骂名；二是借助全国人民反殖民地的激愤之力，通过改换马路名称，赢得民心，造成“接收”的既成事实，以堵住重庆方面的嘴；三是这些马路换上各省、市地名后，这些马路的名字将会永远存在，名垂青史。汪精卫听罢喜上眉梢，立即吩咐上海市长照办。

In 1941, Pacific War broke out and the West led by U.S. became enemies of Japan. The invading Japanese military seized the French Concession, and Wu Kang road fell. In 1943 when the French announced the abandonment of the Concession, Wang Jingwei's puppet government seized the chance to take over the Concession and changed the French Concession around Wu Kang road into the Special Eighth District in Shanghai. Yet the take-over by the Puppet government was accepted neither by the two parties, the Communist and the Kuomintang, nor by the international community. Wang Jingwei was at his wit's end and became sullen and sheltered in Hu Nan Villa. Zhou Fohai and Hu Lancheng came up with a solution and they advised Wang Jingwei to rename the roads with foreign names into names of the counties, cities and provinces of China. Such an act could result in several benefits: first, it could manifest independence, dignity and national integrity of the Puppet government, and help him be rid of the infamy of being a traitor. Secondly, with the anti-colonial sentiment in China, the change of the names of the roads could help

❧湖南别墅的虎皮墙面
the tiger skin like wall

him to win the support from the public. Thirdly, the roads, when named after cities and provinces, would vindicate themselves a permanent place in history. Wang Jingwei had it done immediately.

整个马路更名工作立即进行，办事人员找来当时的全国行政区划图，给租界内的各条马路换上新名。方案形成后由市长亲自送往暂住周佛海湖南别墅的汪精卫审定。汪只对福开森路等几条重要马路给予关注，他凭自己多次途经武康上莫干山留下的美好印象，对周佛海说，武康在山区，福开森路在大都市，但环境和氛围极为相像，不仅洋人喜欢福开森路，上海滩的政要富商都喜欢往那里跑，福开森路就以武康命名吧。武康路从此就在上海滩叫响了。七十多年过去了，这些马路名称沿用至今未被更改，即便是横扫一切的“文革”时期，全国不少城市的街道都被换成与革命有关的称谓，这里也不曾有过任何变动。不管当初汪伪政权的动机如何，也不管他们当年做了多少卖国求荣的事，就这件事而言，并没有做错。

The men in charge of the change embarked on the work instantly and every road was given a new name. When the plan took shape, it was sent to Wang Jingwei who was living then in Zhou Fohai's Hu Nan Villa for approval. Yet Wang was only interested in several important roads, including Avenue Ferguson. He had been to Moganshan several times via Wu Kang and the trips delighted him greatly. Therefore he said to Zhou Fohai, Wu Kang was in the mountainous area, while Avenue Ferguson was metropolitan, yet they do have a lot in common. Not only the foreigners but, the politicians and businessmen love the area there. So why not name it after "Wu Kang" from then on, Wu Kang became a household name in Shanghai. Tens of years went by, yet the names of these roads had not been changed. During the Cultural Revolution, when a lot of streets in Chinese cities were changed into names linked with revolution, everything remained the same here. No matter what was the original motivation of the Puppet government and no matter how traitorous they had been, they did do something right as far as the change of street name is concerned.

如今的武康路全长1,183米，宽12米至16米，聚集着许多名人故居和国家保护建筑。阳光明媚的午后，会看到许多结婚新人在武康路拍结婚照或者广告媒体公司在此取景，整条马路主要是以英国式和西班牙式建筑为主。

而在湖南路和武康路拐角口，就是神秘的湖南别墅。

Right there around the corner of Hu Nan Road and Wu Kang road is the mysterious Hu Nan Villa.

湖南别墅的别样风情
The Scenery of Hu Nan Villa

没有亲自来过湖南路，很难想像在如此热闹的上海滩，在上海的市中心、繁忙的商业区附近，竟然有着这样一条曲折蜿蜒的马路，静若处子，像是普通街巷，没有丝毫张扬的意味。湖南路是上海市区很少的不通公车的马路，这里也是上海著名的情侣路，行人稀少，绿叶遮天，幽静深远。如果两个人可以在这里牵手行走，大约是可以一直走到永远了。蓊郁葱茏的法国梧桐，一栋栋保存完好、静静地裹在阳光中的老别墅、老石库门，无声地延续着。似乎它们都厌倦了浮华掠影的聒噪，独自静卧在这里，享受清幽和安宁。

It is hard to imagine that around downtown in tumultuous Shanghai there should be such a winding road standing quietly there as self-effacing as any other common street in the city. Hu Nan Road is one of the very few streets in Shanghai where there are no buses. Quiet with few pedestrians, it is the most well-known trysting place in Shanghai. Walking here hand in hand, you might feel that you can just walk on and on towards eternity. The lush plane trees and the well-preserved old villas bathed in the sunshine seem to be lasting forever. It seems they are tired of the worldly noise and are just lying here to enjoy this tranquility and peace.

湖南路是跨徐汇区及长宁区的一条街道，东西走向，东起淮海中路，西至华山路，全长1,025米，宽14～19米，车行道宽9～10米，修筑于1918年到1921年，那时以曾任英国驻华公使、经历辛亥革命和袁世凯称帝等事件的英国外交家朱尔典的名字命名为朱尔典路。这里属于上海法租界中段，距淮海中路仅几步之遥。该路沿线为上海法租界西部的高级住宅区，至今仍保留着700余幢花园住宅，居住此区域的多为知名人士和离休干部。赵丹、阮玲玉都曾在这里居住，这些风流人物都为湖南路刻下了别样风情。

Hu Nan Road, an east-west street crossing the border between Xu Hui and Chang Ning districts, starts in the east with Middle Huai Hai Road and ends in the west with Hua Shan Road. Zhao Dan and Ruan Lingyu ever lived here, adding something different to Hu Nan Road.

很难描述这里的静谧与幽雅，街两边伸延着老式弄堂，窄窄的巷子，曲径通幽，各式的洋楼是租界时期留下的遗物，显示出这条街不同寻常的历史。漫步在这空荡的长街上，恍惚中路如其名，仿佛置身于湖南的灵山秀水之间，那种灵气，那种清幽，俯首即是。地图上短短一段距离，走起来却很长。马路两旁的老洋房里装满了老克勒们的风流韵事，泛着银光的留声机上，一张老唱片“吱呀呀”地转着，吟唱着属于老上海的爱情，像张爱玲的书，像阮玲玉的戏。

It is hard to depict the quiet here. The lanes, the narrow paths and diversified villas are all the remains of concession era, showing the unique history behind the street. Wandering in this hollow road, you might feel you are present in picturesque Hu Nan with the unavoidable tranquility. It is much longer than it looks on the map. The villas along the road house the romances of the old upper class and an old record played on the gramophone sings the love story unique in old Shanghai, just like Zhang Ailing's book or Ruan Lingyu's movie.

而这座名为湖南别墅的大宅子，则是一座气派的大宅门，终年紧闭，永远别指望着能进去，半个多世纪以来很少有人进出。外墙用粗石砌成，四周的墙砌得特别高，如今又在已经极高大的围墙上加了一人多高的竹篱笆栅栏，篱笆上长满了爬山虎绿叶，什么都看不到。据说有人曾尝试登上马路正对面六楼公寓的顶楼，但视线还是被竹篱笆和里面的茂密树林完全阻挡住，厚重的深黑色铁门严丝密合得连偷窥的缝都没有，给人一种沉重而且不敢触及之感，那个神秘劲儿令人心跳，高深莫测。铁门边的外墙上烫着“湖南别墅”四个金色大字。无论从哪个角度，都无法全窥它的风貌。

The residence named Hu Nan Villa is an imposing house with the door closed all year round. Few people have ever been there for almost half a century. Built with stones, the surrounding walls are very high. In recent years, bamboo fences higher than man were have been planted on the high walls. And with the fences concealed by the ivy leaves, nothing within can be seen from without. It is said that someone attempted to climb to the top of the six-storied apartment right across the street, only to see the fences and the woods inside. The massive black iron gate, intact without even a crack to look through, makes it even more mysterious and unfathomable. Beside the iron gate, the four Chinese character of Hu Nan Villa are carved in gold. No matter seen from which angle, Hu Nan Villa does not show itself easily.

它建于1931年，是一幢掩藏在浓密的绿荫中的西班牙式独立花园住宅。位于旧时法租界西区的高尚居住区，从建筑与花园的规模、建筑布局与风格特征以及花园与街道的空间关系看，都属于近代上海20世纪二三十年代繁荣

时期典型的独立式花园住宅，折射出当时富裕阶层优裕的生活方式。

Built in 1931, it is an independent Spanish-style garden villa. Located in the upper-class residential area in the west part of French Concession, it was a typical example of the garden house in the prosperous era during the 1920-1930's, judged from the scale of the garden, the layout, the traits and the special relationship between the garden and the street. It embodies the life style of the well-off class of that era.

该住宅由G.O.Wootten建筑师事务所设计，总体为假三层，混合结构。坐北朝南，呈"L"形布局，南向长24.6米，为主立面。主要居室布置在建筑南侧，北侧主要为楼梯间和厨房、卫生间、储藏室等辅助用房。

Designed by the architect G. O. Wootten, the house is a three-storied building with a mixed structure. Facing the South, it is L-shaped with the south facade. The main rooms are arranged in the south of the building and in the north side are mainly the staircase, the kitchen, the bathrooms.

底层为家庭起居活动空间，主要包括：入口门廊、门厅、会客厅、面向花园的敞廊、餐厅和厨房；二层为居住空间，主要包括：主次卧室、起居室、大阳台及东西两侧室外露台；三层阁楼为客房和储藏空间。

The first floor includes the front porch, lobby, the parlor, the open gallery facing the garden ,the dining-room and the kitchen. The second floor is the living space, including the main and secondary bedrooms, living room, balcony and terraces outside the bedrooms on the east and west side. The attic on the top is guest room and storeroom.

住宅的建筑风格显然是西式的，未受到现代建筑风格的影响，在众多上海近代花园洋房中自有其一些独特之处。住宅歇山式屋顶，壁炉烟囱高高耸起。人字形山墙构成南向和东向的主立面。南立面底层敞廊设通常的水平红瓦披檐，楼层与假三层分别为双柱式平拱敞廊与平拱窗，比例尺度精巧，与石砌墙柱形成对比，双坡檐在顶部折为四坡水平檐口。人字形山墙、墙角、窗间壁柱、入口等都以不规则石块砌筑，墙面纹理自然，总之整栋建筑显得豪华气派。

❧爬山虎与墙面融为一体
the ivy and the wall integrated as one

The architecture is without the influence of modern style. Therefore, it is quite unique among the garden villas in modern Shanghai with the irimoya （a hip roof sloping down on all four sides） and the insuppressible chimney. The roof gables form the facades in the south and the east. On the base of the south facade, there is the horizontal red tile slope eaves. The floors and the attic are respectively of double-pillared drop arc corridor and drop arc window, with a perfect proportion and in contrast to

❧湖南别墅面向花园的室外露台
the balcony facing the garden

the stone carved walls. The double slope eaves gradually developed into four slope horizontal cornice. The gables, the corners and the entrance are all carved with random-shaped stones with the very natural texture. All in all, the building looks luxurious and imposing.

南立面四根高耸的实墙柱支撑着二层大阳台，东西两侧墙面高两层，中间两堵实墙在一层半位置收头，上立双柱造型，托起曲线型二层檐板，竖向构图十分强烈。东立面同样有四根墙柱，以一层半的高度承托着露台。露台下是住宅的主入口，直接联系着进厅和主楼梯。

On the south facade, the four solid wall columns support the big balcony on the second floor. The walls on the east and the west are as high as two floors and the two walls in between go inward at the place of one and a half floor. And on top of it double columns are set up to support the curved eave of the second floor. On the east facade are also four wall columns that support the terrace. Under the terrace is the main entrance, connecting the corridor and the main stairs.

这八根墙柱均以石材砌筑，并以水泥勾出凸缝，勾缝砂浆饱满、外凸尖翘，整个“虎皮石”墙面形式粗犷自然，极富雕塑感。除这些石材墙柱外，建筑外墙和窗台板及墙面装饰线均采用乳白色弹涂，也是建筑特色之处。

These eight columns are all built with stones and joints are fashioned on it with concrete. With the joints full of mortar, the tiger-skin like walls are natural and present a strong sense of sculptural beauty. Besides these stone wall columns, the exterior walls and the window sills are painted with white elastic coating, which is also the unique trait of the building.

主楼梯、壁炉、大阳台和露台为该建筑室内主要的特别之处。室内进厅主楼梯为全木雕花楼梯，栏杆以旋拧攀升为造型，采用整木雕琢而成，做工精巧。梯段与踏步，踏步与栏杆，栏杆与扶手之间的搭接利用曲线线角过渡，形式舒展流畅。壁炉设于一层客厅和二层主卧室内，从原始图纸分析，位置恰好在过厅与客厅的分隔墙的正中部位，因而成为整个居住空间的构图中心。从尺度来看，壁炉墙墩厚重，高宽比例舒展，其造型装饰比较华丽考究。据现状判断，可能已为板条墙面封堵。二层大阳台在主卧室南立面一侧，宽3.6米，长近14米，并在东南端向北折回1.8米，是湖南别墅正立面空间、形式和构图的核心，也是整栋别墅造型独特的因素所在。石材墙面顶部以双柱收头也是极富特点的造型元素。

The main staircase, the mantel piece, the balcony and the terrace are the main characteristics of the interior. The staircases in the corridor are all carved wooden stairs with a screw-shaped railing made exquisitely of wood. The lap joint between the stairs and the step and that between the step and the railing is transited in curve, making it free flowing and natural. The mantel piece is set in the parlor on the ground floor and in the main bedroom on the second floor. According to the original blueprint, it should be right in the center of the wall that separates the corridor from the parlor, for it is the very center of the whole building. As far as the size is concerned, the fireplace is solid with a proportional height, polished and furnished splendidly.

周佛海与《色·戒》

Zhou Fohai and *Lust, Caution*

七十多年来，此宅的主人都是与近代中国命运息息相关的大人物，其产权的更迭也像是一段微缩的中国近代历史。湖南别墅在历史沧桑中数易其主，这栋一直作为湖南路风景线的老房子，在经历了上海百年历史巨变后的今天，仍然熠熠生辉。

For more than three score and ten years, the owners of the house have all been the leading figures in the contemporary history of China. The alteration of the ownership is a miniature of the modern history in China. Hu Nan Villa, the landscape on Hu Nan Road, is still standing gorgeously after having experienced

❧湖南别墅的平拱窗
the jack arc window of
Hu Nan Villa

the hundred-year's historical changes.

该宅的建造者原是英商锦隆洋行的一位大股东。太平洋战争爆发后，此宅的主人也许因战争已经回国，也许是被关入了集中营。总之，在撤退前这处房产被变卖了。当时武康路两旁的豪宅别墅急需脱手的很多，时间又紧迫，迫使主人贱卖，而国民政府的要员、商贾富豪，则乘机压低价格大肆收买，转眼间它们都换上了新主人。

The builder of the house used to be a stockholder of Attorneys of the Excess Insurance Company Limited. After the start of Pacific War, the owner either returned home due to the war, or was taken into an interment camp. All in all, the house was sold before the withdrawal. At that time with so many garden villas on sale along Wu

❧湖南别墅的天花顶灯
the ceiling lamp in Hu Nan Villa

Kang road and the urgent situation, a number of foreigners were forced to sell their houses at very low prices. And the officials of Kuomintang and the merchants took the opportunity to buy, and became the new owners overnight.

1940年3月，汪伪政府在南京正式成立，周佛海担任财政部长、警政部长、军事委员会副委员长、上海市长、行政院副院长等要职。1943年春，这位汪伪政权的第三号人物买下了这座花园豪宅作为他在上海的官邸，他和妻子杨淑慧成了该宅的新主人。朱尔典路也随着周的到来而改名为湖南路（周系湖南沅陵人），这栋洋房就被称作“湖南别墅”。

March of 1940 saw the official establishment of the Wang Jingwei's Puppet Government, and Zhou Fohai was the finance minister, the police minister, the mayor of Shanghai and the Vice Chairman of the Military Commission all rolled in one. In the spring of 1943, Zhou Fohai, the third-in-command of the puppet government, bought this garden villa as his mansion in Shanghai. He and his wife, Yang Shuhui, became the new owners of the house. His arrival led to the change of

Route A. Charles Culty into Hu Nan Road （Zhou was from Yuanling, Hunan）, hence Hu Nan Villa.

周佛海的妻子杨淑慧出身上海富商家庭，由于父母极力反对女儿和周佛海的婚事，一度将杨淑慧关在家中。在当年的封建环境下，杨淑慧竟敢和周佛海私奔日本结婚，称得上是非常前卫的女性。

Zhou's wife, Yang Shuhui, was born in a rich merchant family in Shanghai. Because of the parents' disapproval of her marriage with Zhou, she was confined indoors. She was a quite avant garde woman at that time because of her boldness in elopement with Zhou Fohai to Japan to get married.

它曾是汪精卫每次来上海首选下榻的地方，平时，常有日本驻沪派遣军土肥原贤二等高级军官、汪伪政府要员出入，这里的地下室则是一个秘密联络指挥中心。胡兰成是众多前往湖南别墅拜访周佛海的人员中最受特别对待的一个，这不仅仅因为胡兰成是汪伪政府宣传部次长，周佛海需要用他来控制沦陷区的新闻文化出版界，更是因为胡兰成的才气和写得一手好文章，尤其他的妻子张爱玲是当时沪上最出众的美女作家。

Hu Nan Villa was the first choice when Wang Jingwei came to Shanghai. It was also a place frequented by Kenji Doihara, sergeant of Japanese military in Shanghai and the government officials, with the cellar in the villa severing as a secret contact center. Hu Lancheng was the only one of the many visitors that was received with special hospitality. It was so not only because Hu Lancheng was the vice minister of the Propaganda Department but also because Hu was a talented man of letters, especially his wife, Zhang Ailing, who was the best woman writer in Shanghai.

有时胡兰成会带着张爱玲到湖南别墅坐坐，每次周佛海总是既羡慕又妒忌地说："兰成兄，我官比你大，但你艳福比我大。"胡兰成只是以"哈哈哈"大笑算作回答。相传，就是在一次拜访中，张爱玲听到了中统利用美人计，派遣美女郑如萍刺杀汪伪要员丁默村的传奇故事。张爱玲记住了这个凄美的故事，但没有立即动笔。其时，上海文艺界对张爱玲嫁给胡兰成这个在汪伪政权任要职的男人非议颇多。但张爱玲已经听不进去了，自欺欺人地认为爱与政治信仰是可以分开的，爱是不可以附带任何条件的。她说："爱使女人化作蝶，义无反顾扑向火……"张爱玲与胡兰成的婚姻不幸被自己言中，她扑向的是“一团到处燃烧的欲望之火”，胡兰成走到哪里便“滥爱”到哪里，他们的婚姻最终变成一场悲剧。

Sometimes, Hu Lancheng took Zhang Ailing to Hu Nan Villa, and every time Zhou Fohai said to him in admirable and envious tone: “I am superior in office yet inferior in romance”. It is said that it was during one of these visits that Zhang Ailing heard of the legendary story about the assassination of Ding Mocun, an important official in the puppet government, by beautiful Zheng Ruping sent by the Bureau of Investigation and Statistics of the Central Executive Committee. Zhang bore this sad story in mind but did not write it down immediately. At this time the literary community in Shanghai was controversial about the marriage between Hu and Zhang. But Zhang Ailing turned a deaf ear to all this, deceiving herself into believing that love had got nothing to do with politics and that love could exist alone. She even said: “love changed a woman into a butterfly, rushing towards the fire without any hesitation”. In their tragic marriage, the fire she was rushing to was the burning sexual fire. Wherever he went, Hu Lancheng had love affairs, which finally reduced their marriage to a tragedy.

李安曾说：“张爱玲的小说都在写别人的事，只有《色·戒》这部小说是在写自己。28页写了30年，她的心中有很多恨意的。”

Ang Lee once said: “Among all the novels of Zhang Ai ling’s, only *Lust, Caution* is About herself. 28 pages in 30 years, she has got too much hate in her.”

在情欲与爱情、阴谋与情感纠葛的背后，还有张爱玲遗落的爱情与碎梦。30年后，张爱玲在海外写出了这个故事，她把女刺客郑如萍改名王佳芝。

Behind this love and desire, conspiracy and affection, there is also Zhang Ailing’s forgone love and smashed dreams. Thirty years later Zhang Ailing wrote the story and she changed the woman assassin Zheng Ruping into Wang Jiazhi.

70年后，当李安为了拍这部电影来到武康路取景，唏嘘不已，在他眼前，张爱玲、王佳芝的影像交替出现……

Seventy years later when Ang Lee, for the shooting of the film, came to Wu Kang

湖南别墅幽深的庭院
the deep courtyard of Hu Nan Villa

❧湖南别墅门口
the entrance of Hu NanVilla

❧湖南别墅的双柱收头
the double column head in Hu Nan Villa

road, he could not help the mist in the eyes. Zhang Ailing and Wang Jiazhi appeared alternatively before his eyes.

1944年汪精卫死后，周佛海掌握了汪伪政府的大权，竭力扩建特务武装，残酷镇压抗日民众，大肆搜刮民脂民膏，贪污大量钱财。在周佛海担任汪伪政府警政部长和上海市市长期间，实行了白色恐怖和多次“清剿运动”，重庆与日伪双方的谍报战，电影《色·戒》做了惊心动魄的展示。而其妻子杨淑慧是出了名的爱财如命之人，大量贪污得来的钱财自然被杨淑慧一手掌控。

The death of Wang Jingwei in 1944 led to the Zhou Fohai's reign in the puppet government. He cruelly suppressed the Anti-Japanese public and squeezed people to their last drop of blood. During his reign as the police minister and the mayor of Shanghai, he implemented the white terror and carried out numerous large-scaled round-ups. The intelligence activities between Chung King and the puppet government backed by Japan were given a detailed presentation in the movie *Lust,Caution*. Yang Shuhui, Zhou's wife, was a money-grabber and thus was in charge of the bribes.

但周佛海一家在湖南别墅只住了三年多就被赶了出来。1945年8月14日，日本侵略者宣布无条件投降。在全国人民要求严惩汉奸卖国贼的强大压力下，国民党政府不得不将周逮捕，公审公判定为死刑。

The Zhous lived in Hu Nan Villa for three years before they were driven out. On August 14th, 1945, Japan declared unconditional surrender. Under the pressure of people demanding to punish the traitors, Kuomintang was forced to have Zhou arrested and sentenced to death.

生于1897年的周佛海，是中国近现代史上少有的传奇人物，从现在公开的中共党史里可以了解到，他一生三变，反复无常。他于1920年结识陈独秀，参加了共产主义小组，曾经作为赴日本留学生代表，1921年来上海参加中共"一大"会议，算是中国共产党创建人和"一大"代表之一。"一大"会议之后，他赶回日本继续学业，并以优异成绩毕业于日本京都帝国大学。然而，在这段时期，他对共产主义思想产生动摇，从日本回国后，居然叛党而去，很快便投入到蒋介石国民党的怀抱，成为蒋介石的亲信和国民党内的"状元中委"，受蒋政府的聘请回广东等地任职，先后担任国民党宣传部副部长、代部长等职，撰写了大量反共理论文章。1924年，周佛海正式声明脱离共产党，成为蒋政府的重要一员。抗战期间，当抗日战争进入相持阶段，因为对抗日前途丧失信心，他又叛蒋投入日本人怀抱，与汪精卫密谋后，成为汪精卫日伪政府的第三号人物，汪伪政权的"股肱之臣"，做了不折不扣的大汉奸。1945年抗战胜利，汉奸周佛海成为蒋介石的阶下囚，1946年被蒋的高等法院判以死刑，后在周佛海妻子杨淑慧使用周任上海日伪市长时贪污得来的几十根金条疏通关系，改判为无期徒刑。1948年，病死于南京老虎桥军人监狱。他一生三变，朝秦暮楚，的确值得后人玩味和深思。

Born in 1897, Zhou Fohai was a rare legendary figure in the history of modern China. It could be traced that his life was full of ups and downs. In 1920 he got to know Chen Duxiu, took part in the Communist Party and participated in the 1st People's Congress in Shanghai as a representative of the Chinese students in

Japan. To some degree, he was one of the founders of the Communist Party in China and one of the representatives of 1st People's Congress. After the Congress, he returned to Japan and graduated with a distinction from Kyoto Imperial University. However, at this time he began to waver in his political stance. After his return from Japan, he deserted the party and embraced Chiang Kai-shek's Kuomintang. Pretty soon he became the favorite of Chiang Kai-Shek and served in a lot of positions. He successively served as the Vice Minister of the Propaganda Department and the Acting Minister and wrote a lot of anti-Communist articles. In 1924 Zhou Fohai officially announced his breaking away from the Communist and becoming an important member in Chiang's government. When the Anti-Japanese war came to a stage of stalemate, Zhou, losing confidence in the outcome of the war, betrayed Chiang Kai-Shek and took side with the Japanese. The conspiracy with Wang Jingwei found him a complete traitor, ranking the third in the puppet government. The victory of the Anti-Japanese war in 1945 reduced Zhou Fohai to a prisoner and he was sentenced to death by the Supreme Court in the following year. Later on this death penalty was changed into life imprisonment as a result of the dozens of gold bars embezzled by him when he was the mayor of Shanghai. He died in 1948 of illness in the prison. His inconstancy deserves the ruminations of the later generations.

周佛海入狱后，蒋介石并没有太多为难杨淑慧，所以，杨淑慧虽然权力、地位被一扫而空，在上海的日子还是过得非常奢华。新中国建立后，杨淑慧行事更加低调，过着离群索居的隐居生活。1951年，中共中央要确认“一大”会址，上海市公安局很快就查到杨淑慧居所，请她带路寻找中共“一大”会址。因为1921年那会儿，杨淑慧正和周佛海热恋中，两人还曾一起去过中共“一大”会址处几次。杨淑慧长期在上海生活，尽管30年过去了，周围环境变化已经很大，她带着市府人员在兴业路一带来回寻找了数日，终于认出兴业路76号（现在的“新天地”隔壁）就是1921年时中共“一大”会址，市府人员拍下照片送中央高层确认。随后，中共中央再从北京派参加过“一大”会议的李达来现场确认无误。1962年冬，杨淑慧从楼梯上跌下意外死亡。

❧湖南别墅的侧面极富立体感
the dimensional profile of Hu Nan Villa

After the imprisonment of Zhou Fohai, Chiang Kai-Shek did not make life difficult for Yang Shuhui. As a result, though deprived of power and position, she still lived in extravagance in Shanghai. After the founding of New China, she was even more withdrawn. In 1951, the Communist Party wished to locate the site of the 1st People's Congress. The police station in Shanghai found her and asked her to help to find the location. In 1921, when Yang and Zhou were in love, they went to the site of the Congress several times. Although there had been great changes in Shanghai in the past 30 years, Yang Shuhui and the government officials, after several days of searching, finally recognized 76 Xing Ye Road （now next to Xin Tian Di） as the exact site where the 1st Congress, was held. The officials took some pictures of the site and sent them to the state government. Later on the Central Committee sent Li Da, the participator in the

全木雕花楼梯
the wood carved staircase

Congress to Shanghai to confirm the location. In the winter of 1962 Yang Shuhui fell from the stairs and died.

随着周佛海的入狱，湖南别墅也被国民政府接收，成为军统局一个下属机关所在，1946年起作为“中国新社会事业建设协会”总会会址，该会前身是1945年在重庆成立的“人民行动委员会”，两组织都是由蒋介石授意军统局牵头，并合青、洪、袍哥、汉留等派的全国性帮会组织，是军统特务的外围组织。

With the imprisonment of Zhou Fohai, Hu Nan Villa was taken over by the Government and served as a subordinate of the Bureau of Investigation and Statistics. Beginning from 1946 it was used as the site of Social Enterprise Development Association. The predecessor of this association was the people's Action Committee established in Chungking in 1945. Both organizations were authorized by Chiang Kai-Shek and organized by Bureau of Investigation and Statistics through the merging of some nation-wide secret societies.

新中国成立后，湖南别墅被国家没收，邓小平、陈毅两家曾入住此楼，住过一小段时间。当时邓家住在二楼，陈家住在一楼。陈毅后来调往北京外交部工作后，这里就作为上海市委招待所，专门接待中央来沪的高级首长。在此居住时间最长的大概要推贺子珍同志，她的晚年就是在此度过的。

After the liberation, Hu Nan Villa was confiscated. The families of Deng Xiaoping and Chen Yi moved in and stayed some time together in the house, with Deng's family living on the second floor and Chen's on the ground floor. Later on Chen Yi went to Beijing to work in the Ministry of Foreign Affairs, and Hu Nan Villa became the Guesthouse attached to Shanghai Municipal Party to accommodate of state leaders. The one living here for the longest period of time might be He Zizhen, who spent her late life here.

贺子珍放不下的那份深情
The Love that He Zizhen Could Easily not Forego

贺子珍（1909—1984），原名桂圆，又名自珍，江西省永新人，1926年加入中国共产党。曾任共青团永新县委书记、中共吉安县委妇女运动委员会书记。1928年在湘赣边界特委和红四军前委机关做机要和宣传工作，同年与毛泽东结婚，任中共湘赣边特委机关秘书、毛泽东的秘书。1937年冬去前苏联治病，后入莫斯科东方大学学习。

Born in Yongxin, Jiangsu province, He Zizhen, originally named Gui Yuan, joined the Communist Party in 1926. After that she served as the league secretary of Yongxing County Party Committee and the secretary of Women Movement Committee in Ji'an County. In 1928, while working in the border area between Hu Nan and Jiangxi Provinces, she married Mao Zedong and became his secretary as well as secretary of Hunan-Jiangxi Border Special office. In 1937 she went to the former Soviet Union for the treatment and later she studied in Moscow East University.

1954年，贺子珍从前苏联回国就医，据说她在前苏联的日子比长征还苦，甚至被不分青红皂白地送进了精神病医院。在接受组织安排来到上海，担任虹口区组织部部长期间，她曾对一位老战友说：“不要因为我曾是‘第一夫人’而把我禁起来，希望能见一见老毛，说句话、握个手就行。”贺子珍到了上海后，毛泽东对陈毅说，“子珍在上海的生活从我的稿费中支出”。陈毅则说，“上海养得起一个贺子珍”。

In 1954 He Zizhen returned from the former Soviet Union for medical treatment. It is reported that her life in the former Soviet Union was harder than the Long March and she was even sent to a mental hospital for no reason at all. When sent to Shanghai to be the minister of the Organization Department of Hong Kou District, she said to an old friend: “Don't confine me indoors because I was the first lady, I only hope to see him and chat with him, even a handshake is enough”. After she came to Shanghai, Mao Zedong said to Chen Yi: “Her expenses in Shanghai will be paid from my contribution fees.” Chen Yi said: “Shanghai is capable of providing for He Zizhen.”

1950年，彭儒到上海看贺子珍，还笑过她：“哎，你怎么养起猪来了！”的确，贺子珍和彭儒这些女学生出身的老干部，是不大有养猪经验的。不过贺子珍每天用水龙头给猪洗澡，把猪收拾得可干净了。

❧湖南别墅厚重的门把手
the doorknob of Hu Nan Villa

湖南别墅室内
the interior of Hu Nan Villa

In 1950, Peng Ru came to visit He Zizhen in Shanghai and laughed at her "How come you raise a pig". Indeed, these students-turned cadres did not know how to raise a pig. She gave the pig a shower every day and it was really a clean pig.

尽管毛泽东来上海时经常居住在距离几步之遥的兴国宾馆一号楼，但是从公开的资料里可以了解，他们在上海从没有见过面。仅有的一次记载是1959年，贺子珍上庐山和毛主席见过一次面，谈话一个多小时。

Every time when Mao Zedong came to Shanghai, he would stay in Villa One a few steps away. Yet the record showed that they had never met each other. The only meeting was the one on Lushan where they saw each other and talked for an hour.

在上海的几十年间，贺子珍搬过5次家，湖南别墅是最后一处，既是她居住时间最长的，也是贺子珍的外孙女孔东梅最熟悉的居所：从1972年在上海出生到1979年随妈妈李敏回北京，孔东梅都是在此与贺子珍共同生活。在她的回忆里，湖南别墅的院子很大，种满橘树，到了秋天可以结几百斤果子。言语不多的外婆，偶然身体好些的时候，会教孔东梅在院子里种花草。湖南路住所可比溧阳路住所大多了，但20年过去，贺子珍毕竟老了。她能做的就是和女儿李敏一起在玉兰树下拔去杂草，在花坛前闻闻花香。

During her dozens of years residing in Shanghai, He Zizhen moved five times and Hu Nan Villa, the last residence, was also the one her granddaughter, Kong Dongmei, was most familiar with. From her birth in Shanghai in 1972 till her return to Beijing in 1979 with her mother Li Min, Kong Dongmei lived there with her grandmother. In her memory, there was a large yard of orange trees in the Hu Nan Villa. In the autumn, the trees could produce hundreds of kilograms of fruits. When health permitted, the grandmother would teach her to grow flowers in the yard. The residence on Hu Nan Road was much larger than the one on Li Yang Road, yet 20 years saw He Zizhen getting old. All she could do was to pull weeds under the magnolia trees and enjoy the flowers in the yard.

孔东梅记忆最深刻的事，是放学回家，到家门口时，由于自己个子矮，够不着门铃，天天把小书包垫在脚底下按门铃的情景。在那里的几年，她真有些寂寞锁深宫的感觉，只要回了家，就很难出门，而且也不能带小朋友回家玩。门口总有警卫员把守，她的最叛逆的记录也不过是偷偷跑到对面马路买根5分钱的冰棍。

Kong Dongmei could always remember the time when she came back from school. She had to stand on her school bag to ring the bell for she was short. In those years she felt lonely because she could not go out as long as she got home and she could not invite little friends home. In addition, there were always guards at the gate. The most rebellious thing she could remember was stealing out to buy a popsicle on the other side of the street.

那时，贺子珍经常带几个孩子去串门，大人在屋里聊天，两家的孩子就在外面那巨大的草坪上玩耍。由于常来常往，亲如一家，大家都没想起要正正经经照个相什么的。对于湖南别墅，孔东梅有过这样的描述：这幢房子有两个特点，一是隐蔽，这对于幽居上海的外婆来说，确实保密性很好；二是有一个面积超乎想像的庭院，包括约两个网球场大的草坪，栽满了花草树木，一棵白玉兰亭亭玉立，两栋楼房分别为外婆和工作人员居住，被假山、花园、水池所环绕。

Sometimes He Zizhen had her friends over. When the adult chatted in the house, the children would play on the vast lawn. They were as close as a family and it never occurred to them to take a picture together. Kong Dongmei described the villa as having two features: the one is that it is well-concealed, so it could not be better for grandmother; the other is that there is an incredibly large courtyard, including a lawn as large as two tennis courts with flowers and trees, including a magnolia tree. The two houses, surrounded by garden and ponds, was home to grandmother and the working staff.

贺子珍在湖南别墅的生活，每天都很有规律，清早起来在院子里散步、打太极拳，吃过早饭就翻看报纸，吃过中饭午睡2小时，起床后就在园子里干活，不是浇水就是拔草，累得满头大汗。晚饭后，一般早早上床，搂着外孙女孔东梅讲故事。有时，李敏从北京回来，告诉她许多有关北京和毛泽东的事，她就听得特别仔细，有时还会刨根问底。每逢有毛泽东托李敏带回书信和礼物，她就特别开心，打开后门来到优雅清静的武康路散步。她们一边走一边聊，一直走到武康路与霞飞路交叉口的宋庆龄住处，然后又折回来。

每次经过路边的小店，贺子珍总忘不了给身边的工作人员带点吃的回来。有一次，她问李敏武康路有多长?李敏答不上来，贺子珍就把自己掌握的数字报了出来，她还特别告诉李敏，没有人告诉她武康路的长度，是她自己用脚步量出来的，她每步50厘米，十分精确。这些年她天天沿着院子兜圈子，除了数步子还是数步子，功夫就这么练成的。

He Zizhen lived a very routine life in the villa: in the morning, a walk and Tai Chi and newspaper reading after the breakfast; a two-hour nap after lunch and some work in the garden; and story time with the granddaughter after the supper. Sometimes Li Min came back from Beijing and brought back information about Beijing and Mao Zedong and she listened carefully. Whenever Li Min brought back

❧湖南别墅一楼会客室
the parlor of the first floor

letters and gifts from Mao Zedong, she would be very happy and would take a walk with the daughter till they came to the crossing of Wu Kang Road and Avenue Joffre where Soong Ching-ling lived. On the way back, she would always buy some delicacy for the staff. Once she asked Li Min how long the Wu Kang Road was and Li Min had no idea. He Zizhen told her the length and she measured that with her own feet. All these years she walked every day in the yard and year after year she walked with a step as exact as 50 centimeters.

1966年“文革”初期，毛泽东在天安门广场接见红卫兵的新闻传到了湖南别墅，这使得思念毛泽东心切的贺子珍突发奇想，要求搭乘红卫兵进京列车去天安门广场见毛泽东。身边的工作人员连忙劝阻她说：组织上规定不能进京的纪律没有解除，要她服从纪律。满头花白的贺子珍不说话，坐在写字台前一支接一支抽烟，眼睛望着北方陷入了沉思……因为设想的北京之行受阻，1967年她大病一场。到1969年中秋，贺子珍已年届花甲了。

In the dawn of the Cultural Revolution in 1966, the news that Mao Zedong met the Red Guards at Tian An Men Square reached Hu Nan Villa. He Zizhen, missing Mao so much, decided to go to Beijing. The staff around her tried to stop her by saying that the ban that she could not go to Beijing was not lifted yet. He Zizhen did not say anything and just smoked one cigarette after another, lost in meditation with her eyes staring at the north. Because of the aborted Beijing trip, she fell ill in 1967. The arrival of the mid-autumn festival saw He Zizhen an old woman of 60.

需要说明的是：尽管贺子珍住过15年之久，湖南路262号的性质却一直是招待所。这里的服务人员都是从毛泽东来沪时住的兴国宾馆派来的。既然是招待所，吃饭就要收费。贺子珍的标准是每天3元，李敏等人的标准是每天1.5元。每天的伙食费到月底一起结账，从工资中开支。除了贺子珍工资高些，这对大家都是一笔不小的费用。

Though He Zizhen lived there for 15 years, the Hu Nan Villa was in effect still a guesthouse, with the working staff sent by the Xing Guo Hotel. Since it was a guesthouse, meals should be paid for. He Zizhen's dietary standard was 3 Yuan a day while others', Li Min included, was 1.5 Yuan. At the end of the month the monthly meal expenses would be paid from the salary. Except for He Zizhen who

湖南别墅的二楼阳台
the porch on the second floor

湖南别墅二楼卧室
the bedroom on the second floor

had a comparatively higher income, this was not a small amount for the others.

在孔东梅的记忆中，儿时的她特别喜欢和湖南别墅的工作人员玩，吃饭时也常跑到他们的大灶，好像那里的饭菜特别香。这些叔叔、阿姨中，她一直记得贺子珍身边的工作人员小韩叔叔。1977年贺子珍中风之后住进华东医院。直到去世，7年里她再没回过湖南路。既然她不在这里住了，身边工作人员也裁减了，但韩叔叔一直留了下来。等到1984年贺子珍去世，后事处理完毕，他才离开。

In Kong Dongmei's memory, she loved to stay with the staff and have meals with them as if their meal tasted better, among whom she in particular remembered an Uncle Han. In 1977 He Zizhen had a stroke and lived in Huadong Hospital until her death. For seven years she had never been back to the house on Hu Nan Road and some of staff were dismissed. But uncle Han stayed until the death of He Zizhen and he left only after all the things had been properly dealt with.

小韩叔叔名叫韩洪高，大家都叫他小韩，苏北人，文化水平不高，但性格爽直，喜欢和小孩子逗着玩。他给孔东梅的印象是：像个“大管家”，说话声音很大，“凶凶”的，力气也大。一辆“二八”男车，小韩叔叔一只手就能高高举起来，转着圈让大家看，让小孩子们惊奇得不得了。骑着这辆车，小韩叔叔经常带孔东梅出去办事。“在自行车后座上，能看到外边的世界，那么多有意思的事情，我非常开心”。

Uncle Han was properly named Han Honggao and people just called him Han Coming from Jiangsu. Not educated, he was straight forward and loved to play with kids. In Kong Dongmei's memory he was like the butler, loud and speaking and fearful. He was also quite strong and could lift a bicycle with one hand, which greatly amazed the children. When on errands, uncle Han often took Kong Dongmei. “Sitting at the back of the bike, I was very happy to see the world outside.” Kong Dongmei said.

院子里的假山、花园是孔东梅童年记忆中神奇的所在，觉得里面藏着无穷秘密。春天有玉兰，夏天有池水，秋天有蝉蜕，冬天有腊梅——贺子珍不让别人摘，小东梅摘她不管。蝉蜕可以入药，小韩叔叔和小东梅一起捡过好多，卖给药铺，得了一笔小小的财富。用这笔劳动所得，小韩叔叔给小东梅

❧湖南别墅通往阁楼的楼梯
the staircase leading to the attic

买了铅笔盒、橡皮等文具，让她兴奋了大半年。

The rockeries and the garden were a miracle in Kong's memory, revealing to her lots of secrets. In the spring time there is the magnolia tree, in summer there is the pond; in the fall there is the cicada; and when winter comes there is the winter sweet which only little Dongmei could pick. Cicada slough could serve as a medicine and she, together with uncle Han, would find a lot and get money by selling them to a drug store. With this money, uncle Han would buy some stationery such as eraser and pencil box which delighted her for more than half a year.

一次，二楼屋顶落下一只黄鹂。小韩叔叔冒险爬上房顶把它捉住，养了起来。后来鸟死了，小韩叔叔又把它做成标本。再后来，标本也不见了。是带回北京后不见的，还是在上海就不见的？孔东梅记不清了。

Once an oriole fell on the roof and uncle Han climbed up to catch it. Later the bird died and Han made it into a specimen. Later even this specimen was gone. Kong Dongmei could not remember whether it was lost in Beijing or Shanghai.

孔东梅还记得：院子里跑来一只波斯猫，不知谁家的，白白的，可爱极了。猫成了她的心肝宝贝，天天抱着。养了几个月后，有一天猫不见了，她急得三天不吃不睡。大人都说：跑丢了，跑丢了。后来才知道：小韩叔叔给它洗澡，用水龙头直接冲。猫耳朵进了水，小波斯猫就死了！

She also remembered once a white Persian cat came into the yard. She just loved it and carried it every day. One day it disappeared and she was so sad that she could not eat or sleep for three days. Adults said that it simply run away. Only later on did she learn that it died with water in its ears when uncle Han was giving it a shower.

2004年2月，孔东梅陪妈妈李敏再次回到湖南路262号。当年在这里工作过的人们都已白发苍苍，大家又聚在了一起。小韩叔叔没有来——他前些年回了苏北老家，得癌症去世了。“小韩叔叔是个粗人，但是个好人——我认为”。

In February, 2004, Kong Dongmei accompanied her mother back to Hu Nan Villa. They had a get-together with the people who had ever worked here, all of whom were old. Uncle Han was absent, because he died years ago from cancer at home.

"Uncle Han was uneducated, yet he was a good man, I think", Kong said.

的确，离开湖南别墅后，孔东梅再也没有养过那样让自己心疼的小猫咪，再也没有进过那样让自己着迷的假山花园，没有用过那样让自己兴奋和珍惜的铅笔盒。湖南别墅是孤寂的，又是有趣的。那些与外婆贺子珍在一起的日子，从来没有离她远去过。每当想起外婆贺子珍，她都会想起湖南路的大院子，想起白发苍苍的贺子珍坐在写字台前的椅子上，一枝一枝抽着烟，面向绿草如茵的窗外，望着远方沉思的样子。

Indeed, after she left Hu Nan Road, Kong Dongmei never raised any cat that cute, never entered the garden that enchanting and never used the pencil box that precious. Life in Hu Nan Road was lonely, but fun as well. Life there with grandmother never left her. Whenever she thought about the grandmother, she would recall the grey-haired He Zizhen sitting at the table with cigarette one after another, lost in meditation.

也就是在湖南路，当时4岁的孔东梅在朦朦胧胧中觉得世界上发生了一件大事。

It is also here in Hu Nan Road that four-year-old Kong Dongmei realized dimly that something big happened in the world.

"那天大人们的神情很反常，海峰姨跑到外婆房间里痛哭失声。她拿着一条大毛巾频频拭泪，那种湿乎乎的感觉我至今记得。外婆则叉着腰，急促地走来走去。后来我知道，那天就是1976年9月9日。外公于当天凌晨去世，消息下午已传遍全国，也终于传到了湖南路。"

"On that day, the adults were very strange and Aunt Haifeng rushed into He Zizhen's room and cried. She took a towel and constantly removed her tears. And grandmother walked back and forth in the room with her arms akimbo. Later on I got to know that lt was September 9th, 1976 and it was on the dawn of that day that grandfather passed away. In the afternoon the news had spread throughout the country and it finally reached Hu Nan Road."

然而那天，贺子珍的反应出人意料，异常冷静。她只是反复自言自语：主席身体不是很好吗？怎么，一下子就走了？显然，李敏没有把毛泽东病危的实情告诉她。此时的李敏悲痛欲绝，大家从电视上发现她哭得"眼都直

❧湖南别墅阁楼
the attic in Hu Nan Villa

了”。但她还是想到了自己的母亲贺子珍，请自己的丈夫赶来上海照料。

But He Zizhen's reaction on that day was unexpected and extremely calm. She repeatedly said to herself: "Chairman has always been healthy, how come that he passed away so suddenly." It was apparent that Li Min kept her in dark about the illness of Mao Zedong. At that time Li Min was in great sorrow and every one could see on TV that she had cried too much. Yet she still thought about the mother and asked her husband to Shanghai to take care of her.

“经过妈妈尽力争取，外公的长女有了在人民大

❧湖南别墅的参天老树
the old trees

会堂守灵一天的权利。我也被爸爸接到北京，来到外公遗体前，参加了那一天的守灵。当时，我只知有外婆，不知有外公，更不会把眼前这位长眠的老人与自己的亲人联系在一起。但是，据妈妈说我那天却哭得昏天黑地，是被大人抱出来的。为什么？谁也说不清。也许，我在那一天意识到了‘死亡’这一概念。很多人告诉我，他们是从那一天觉得世界从此不同并开始长大的。”

“Through my mother’s efforts, my mother, the eldest daughter of grandfather, was entitled to a day’s vigil in the Great Hall of the People. I was taken to Beijing by my father for the vigil. At that time I did not know that I had a grandfather and I never thought that the old man lying there had anything to do with me. But according to my mother I cried so hard that day that I was carried out from the hall. No one could account for that. Maybe it was on that day that I first got to know about death. A lot of people told me it was exactly that day that made them feel different and mature.”

这样一所特殊人物居住的特殊宅院，在“文革”期间，会不会像上海其他名人故居那样被洗劫一空呢？据说湖南路及其邻近的武康路一带曾是抄家风潮最盛的地区，因为那里的花园洋房和“黑帮分子”最集中。不过李敏回忆说：“抄家的来过一次，没拿走多少东西，而且很快就原物退还了。”

Could such a house, home to such special people, be ransacked just like other former houses of celebrities during the Cultural Revolution? It is said that the area around Hu Nan Road and Wu Kang Road used to be the target because it was the place where the “anti-revolutionaries” gathered. But according to Li Min: “They did come to the house and took few items away, but they returned the items pretty soon”.

那么贺子珍呢，她当真在“文革”中没有受到明枪暗箭的威胁吗？据孔东梅所知，长期在毛泽东身边工作的汪东兴曾提到这样一件事：“在‘文革’中，陈伯达就来找我，说要把贺子珍从上海搞到西北去。我就对陈伯达说，你是要我转报，还是要我通知毛主席有人要向他报告。陈伯达不敢去主席那里报告，连忙说：‘由你转报最好。’这样，我就向毛主席报告了。”

Then what about He Zizhen. Was she really immune from the threat during the Cultural Revolution? According to Kong Dongmei, Wang Dongxing, who had long been working with Mao Zedong, mentioned that something: “During the Cultural Revolution, Chen Boda came to me and said that they decided to send He Zizhen to the Northwest. I asked him whether he wished to talk about it with the Chairman himself or he wished me to takc the massage for him. He dared not see the Chairman and asked me to do that for him. So I did.

据汪东兴回忆，毛泽东得知后当场沉下脸来说：“我不同意，这是谁出的主意？他们有本事他们干，我不同意……”他把毛泽东的话转告陈伯达，贺子珍才能安静的待在上海。

According to the Wang Dongxing, when Mao Zedong heard it, he was angry at once, saying: “I do not approve of it, who came up with the idea?” He reported back to Chen Boda what the Chairman had said. As a result, He Zizhen stayed in Shanghai.

现在看来，所谓要把贺子珍从上海搞到西北去，背景很像是1969年国庆前后的全国大疏散。当时中苏关系空前紧张，两国冲突一触即发。中共中央

安排包括主席、总理、林彪在内的领导人到外地暂住一段时间，以防止意外损失。无论如何，贺子珍在不知不觉中，在毛泽东的坚决保护下，避开了令人恐慌的大疏散，继续在湖南别墅安度晚年。这不能不说是个奇迹。贺子珍一直安静地居住在湖南别墅里，直到1984年离开人世，其间经历了整个“文革”十年、毛泽东去世和“四人帮”倒台。

Considered now, the idea about moving He Zizhen from Shanghai to the Northwest was very similar to the national evacuation around the National day in 1969. At that time the Sino-Soviet relationship was at a low ebb and it seemed that the bilateral conflict was on the verge of breaking out. The central government made the arrangement that the leaders, including the Chairman, the Premier and Lin Biao, should stay a way from Beijing for some time. Anyway, He Zizhen unconsciously avoided the frightening evacuation under the protection of Mao Zedong and continued her peaceful life in Hu Nan Villa. This was nothing short of a miracle. She stayed in the Villa until her death in 1984. During this period

❧玉兰花开
magnolia in blossom

of time some earth-shaking events happened, such as the ten-year Cultural Revolution, the death of Mao Zedong and the topple of the Gang of Four.

虽然“文革”中江青粉墨登场，权倾一时，顶着革命文艺旗手的光环，大开杀戒整死整残一大批高官和著名演艺界人士，但是从不敢去湖南别墅撒野。“四人帮”中的其余三人，即使都是当时上海响当当的第一二把手，也没有胆量去湖南别墅闹事。

Though the Cultural Revolution gave Jiang Qing the overwhelming power to murder a large group of officials and celebrities, she never dared to approach the Hu Nan Villa. The other three in the Gang of Four, though bossing in Shanghai, stayed away from Hu Nan Villa.

粉碎“四人帮”后的1979年6月11日，《人民日报》刊发消息：全国政协五届二次会议决定增补贺子珍等人为全国政协委员。同时配发了一张照片：一位面颊丰腴、白发苍苍的老人，慈祥地坐在轮椅上，和一个小女孩一起看画报。这位老人就是贺子珍，小女孩则是她的外孙女孔东梅。于是，“贺子珍还活着”的消息在全国引起了强烈震动，雪花似的慰问信飞进贺子珍在湖南别墅的家。

On June 11th, 1979, after the topple of the Gang of Four, People's Daily published the news that He Zizhen was added as a member of the Chinese People's Political Consultative Conference, with a picture enclosed in the report: a silver-haired old woman sitting on a wheelchair, reading a magazine with a little girl. The old woman was He Zizhen and the little girl beside her was her granddaughter, Kong Dongmei. The news that He Zizhen was still alive caused great sensation and letters of consolation rushed towards her house in Hu Nan Villa from all over the country.

1979年9月，中央把贺子珍接到了北京。9月9日是毛泽东的忌日，她献给毛泽东花圈上的落款是“战友贺子珍”。当她离开时，留下了一个回眸，是那样的情意深长……

In September 1979, He Zizhen was taken to Beijing. On the 9th of September which was the death anniversary of Mao Zedong, she dedicated a wreath in the name of He Zizhen, comrades-in-arms. At the moment of leaving, she glanced back, with nothing said yet everything revealed.

回到湖南别墅不久，贺子珍开始生病。在贺子珍生命中，最后7年是在上海华东医院里度过的。1984年她病情恶化，4月15日，李敏通宵达旦地守候在贺子珍身边，18日下午，她从昏迷中突然醒来，握着她与毛泽东唯一的女儿李敏的手说："我好好的，你为什么要流泪呢？我已经看到你爸爸向我点头微笑。"其实这是回光返照。等到19日下午，贺子珍的脉搏越来越弱，最后心电图没有显示了，她，终于停止了心脏跳动。这位伟大的女性、历史的亲历者，用沉默走完了自己的人生。享年75岁，骨灰安放在八宝山革命公墓。

Soon after her return to the Hu Nan Villa, He Zizhen fell ill. The last seven years of her life was spent in Huadong Hospital. In 1984 her condition worsened and Li Min stayed with her day and night on April 15th. On the afternoon of 18th, she suddenly awoke from coma, took the hand of Li Min, her only daughter with Mao Zedong, and said: "I am fine, why cry? I saw your father smiling at me." In the afternoon of 19th, her pulse was getting weaker and weaker and the heart stopped beating. This great woman lived her entire 75 years in silence and her ashes was placed in Ba Bao Shan Revolutionary Cemetery.

也许，有一种放不下的情感，在这座别墅里深深埋藏了数年之久。深深的院子里，种植的都是毛泽东生前喜欢的梅花、榆树和石榴等。想来，在贺子珍的心里，只装着一个人。

Maybe here the house bears witness to an affection deeply concealed. Here in the yard, the plum flower, the elm and the pomegranates were all favorites of Mao Zedong. In He Zizhen's heart there was one and the only one.

继续神秘、低调着
Going on with Mystery and Modesty

现在，这里是兴国宾馆的分部，从大门口一眼望去，丝毫看不见别墅的踪影。路边雪白的墙上挂着青黑色的法式壁灯，旁边赫然就是262号的门牌号。平常日子里，两扇大铁门紧紧关闭着，墙里的梧桐树高大茂盛，早已探过了围墙的高度，墙内墙外的梧桐枝叶搭在了一起。

Now Hu Nan Villa is part of Xing Guo Hotel. A look through the gate will not give you the sight of the villa. French style wall lamps are hanging on the white wall, and beside the lamp is the 262 doorplate. The gates, on common days,are closed tightly. The plane trees within have grown higher than the walls and tangled with the trees without.

花园内有一个小池塘，在小假山上安置了好些瓷鹅之类的装饰物。盆栽的紫藤，生气旺盛。院子左边是一个布局精巧别致、郁郁葱葱的花园，种着梅树、榆树、黄杨树、石榴树、海棠等等，四季花开不断。每逢开花时节，香飘庭院，十分怡人。院墙上方竖起的竹篱笆栅栏，既与外界空间隔开，又让别墅内外树木互相交融，平添了一份乡村风情。

There is a pond in the garden and the rockeries in it were decorated with all kinds of ornaments including procelain geese. The potted ivy looks quite thriving. In the left side of the yard is an exquisitely-designed garden with plum trees, elms box trees, pomegranates and cherry-apple trees, etc. In the blossoming season, the yard is fragrant and appealing. The bamboo fences on the walls, on the one hand, separate the within from the without, and on the other hand, create a harmony between the trees inside and those outside.

院子右边是一条向里延伸的整洁宽敞的私家车道，幽深幽深的庭院，只有耐着性子，沿着弧线车道一路进入，慢慢地走，才发现了里面的妙趣天成。那一刻，真有一种侯门深似海的错觉。原来这门前的园子像是天然的玄关，只是迎客，却不教外人瞥见里面的一分一毫。一直走到院子的最深处，才能看到一幢被梧桐树荫掩映住的大宅子。窗边藤蔓缠绕，寂寂无声。

In the right side is a neat and wide private vehicle lane that seems endless. Only when walking along the curved drive patiently can you be finally rewarded with the heavenly scene. At that moment you will have the sense of displacement. The garden in the front is a hallway, receiving the guests yet not giving them any glimpse of the inside. Only when you come to the further end of the yard, can you see the house itself, concealed and silent among the plane trees.

今天的湖南路依旧很静，幽僻淡静，出尘离世，没有半点市井喧哗，似乎一下远离了纷扰的十里洋场。路两边都是高大的法国梧桐，枝繁叶茂，遮云蔽日，路上行人稀少，偶有车辆过去，一呼而过的声音在这里似乎都有回音。若是下起点零星小雨，细雨洗润过的梧桐叶青翠逼人，路上寥无人声，安静得让人感到空旷。可以想像当年居住此间的人们之神秘、低调。窗帘是

❧掩映在浓密绿荫中的窗口
the window concealed in the thick shade

终日拉下来的，树和花园挡住了他们宅子的窗户，也遮住了他们的生活。

Today’s Hu Nan Road, with the shading planes trees and the few pedestrians, is still quiet, far from the madding crowd. It is so quiet here that an occasionally passing car might cause echoes. On rainy days, with the trees even greener and the street even quieter, one might have the illusion that he was in the wilderness. With the curtain drawn and the windows concealed by the trees and gardens, people who used to live here withdrew their life away from the public attention.

雍福會
The YongFoo Élite

雍福会：奢侈的、神秘的、传说中的东方情调

Yongfoo Elite: The Luxurious and Mysterious East

永福路200号

200 Yong Fu Road

2004年度全球最佳设计会所第二名

The second on the list of 2004 Global Best Design Clubs.

❧雍福会入口

the entrance to Yongfoo Elite

雍福会，现在由兴国宾馆租赁给其他公司经营——这个上海富人圈子里风头正劲的私人会所，藏身于幽静的永福路。两旁古木参天，路上人烟稀少，互相衬托着这座城市中的别样风情。无事在这样的路上闲走也是很写意的，虽没有江南的画意，多的是旧日上海的摩登优雅。

Yongfoo Elite, the most popular club among the rich in Shanghai, lies in the solitary Yong Fu Road. The towering trees and the quiet street create a different world in this modern city. A leisure walk in the street is very romantic in itself, surrounded by the modernness and elegance of old Shanghai.

18世纪前英国文豪约翰逊的那句话——“当一个人厌倦了伦敦时，他也就厌倦了人生。因为伦敦有人生能赋予的一切。”充满着日不落帝国公民的豪情与满足。几百年后，当人们再次审视这个世界，会发现这句话依旧经典，只是，从严格意义上说，它更适合上海，更适合雍福会。在雍福会，一位来自华尔街的外国人惊叹，“它正是我想像中会在上海找到的东西”。

Samuel Johnson, a British writer from the 18th century, once said “when a man is tired of London, he is tired of life; for there is in London all that life can afford.” His words were full of the pride and satisfaction of a citizen in the kingdom where the sun never set. Hundreds of years later, people can still find the sentence classic. However, strictly speaking, it fits Shanghai well and it fits Yongfoo Elite even better. In Yongfoo Elite, a foreigner from New York was marveled, “this is exactly what I thought I would find in Shanghai”.

一草一木渗透古今

The Place Where the Old Meet the New

这座占地3亩（2000平方米）的西班牙风格两层老式洋房，坐落在上海市中心的宁静领馆区，也就是百年前的法租界内。它建于20世纪30年代，几经变迁。最早前的20世纪50年代，这里曾是瑞金医院名医邝安坤的官邸，邝安坤是我国内分泌学科的奠基人之一，早年赴法国留学，获得医学博士学位，法国政府曾授予其法兰西共和国骑士勋章。后来又曾是前苏联、德国、越南领事馆的旧址，1980年代后的21年间则是英国领事馆的所在地，它达观

形式古朴的大缸
the primitive vat

❧雍福会花园里的鸦片床
the opium bed in the garden of Yongfoo Elite

瑰丽的外表中一直渗出特有的“洋味儿”。

Covering an area of 2000 square meters, this Spanish-style two-storied villa lies in the quiet consular district, which used to be within the bounds of Shanghai French Concession. Built in 1930s, this building has gone through many changes. As early as 1950s, it was the residence of Kuang Ankun, a famous doctor from Rui Jin Hospital and one of the founders in Endocrinology in China. In his early years, he studied and graduated with a Doctor's

Degree in Medicine in France, awarded the Knight Badge of the Republic of France by the French government. Later the building was used as the consulates for the former Soviet Union, Germany as well as Vietnam. Beginning from 1980, it served as the British Consulate for as long as 21 years.

上海第一代服装设计师汪兴政先生把它租下来后，用了三年时间精心策划和精打细凿，成为一个私人高级社交中心会员制酒店会所——雍福会之后，它俨然已是一家近乎博物馆的花园餐厅，欧式风格的装修，纯中国式的老家具、老摆设，无处不透着不事张扬的旧日贵族气息。在雍福会，那些匾额、对联很有讲究，红木、青瓷、老皮壳和汉白玉，不但分材质，还要看年份、笔法和执笔人的名头。一草一木均渗透着古今、东西各异的文化气质，又仿佛浑然天成的一件艺术品。“我喜欢将一些原本毫无关联的东西放到一起，西方的、东方的、现代的、古典的，任由它们相互作用”。很多名流、国外高官对此情有独钟。其匠心独特的设计，在上海乃至中国堪称独一无二。在2004年全球评比中它得到最佳会所第二名。

Wang Xingzheng, one of the first fashion designers in Shanghai, rented it and turned it into a private hotel-style membership club, Yongfoo Elite. It is a museum like garden restaurant, with the European decoration and typical Chinese furnishing. In Yongoo Elite, plaque, couplets are quite an art. They are different not only in material but in age, calligraphy and reputation of the writer. Here the old and the new, the West and the East meet and mix so naturally that it is more like a gift from God. "I love to put together things that are unrelated at all". A number of celebrities and foreign officials just love it. It is with no doubt the one and the only one in China and the world as well.

据说在没有见到雍福会前，世界权威性时尚、设计杂志《Wallpaper》已经把非洲一家会所评为“2004年全球最佳设计会所”，看到雍福会后，他们又破天荒地增加了这一奖项的名额，形容雍福会是中国新精英的根据地，并将此荣誉授予了雍福会。

It is said that before seeing Yongfoo Elite, *Wallpaper*, the authority in design, had already rated a club in Africa as the 2004 Global Best Design Club. Yet after they saw Yongfoo Elite, they unprecedentedly added a quota for this award. They depicted Yongfoo Elite as the base of the new elites in China and awarded the honor to Yongfoo Elite.

汪兴政是个典型的上海老克勒，有着一种莫名的贵族品位。他1953年出生于上海，新中国成立前，汪兴政的家里是做丝绸生意的，所以他从小对布料有一些了解。“文革”时他也参加了一些剪裁培训班，所以后来就自己尝试做一些衣服，由淮海路上一家名为“调剂商店”的商场里代卖，没想到那批衣服被一抢而空。他创办服装厂时拿到的私营企业营业执照，是上海市卢湾区的第007号，他是名副其实的中国改革开放以后第一批民营企业家。

With some sort of noble refinement in his Carriage, Wang Xingzheng is a cognoscente in luxury and taste. Born in 1953 in Shanghai into a family that used to do silk business before liberation, he knew cloth well even as a kid. During the Cultural Revolution he took part in tailoring training and made some attempts in clothes making. He ever took the clothes he had made to a market and it turned out that they were sold out immediately. He founded his own clothing factory and was one of the first generation of private entrepreneurs.

❧ 雍福会的下午茶时光
afternoon tea in Yongfoo Elite

他创办的服装品牌“尊龙”，到20世纪80年代后期，在全国拥有三四十个专卖店，在中国人刚刚流行蝙蝠衫、牛仔裤的年代，就成为那时少数国产高端服装品牌之一。这位第一代华人服装设计师每星期必做的两件事情之一便是买衣服，他必须有足够的衣服来满足着装的更新周期。因为他从不以重复的着装示人，而且风格务必特立独行。为此他不仅常常为自己做衣服，还喜欢把买来的衣服换上自己从国外的古玩市场淘来的古董纽扣。对诸如此类大费周章的事情汪兴政却乐在其中，他永远沉溺于自己“偏执”的美学准则中。他买衣服时，尽量不看品牌，据说这样更能够增加识别能力，少一些误导。“穿衣服到现在，从来没有发现跟我撞衫的人”。

He created his own brand Johnlone, and till the late of

1980s he occupied forty exclusive shops throughout the country. At the time when batwing coats and jeans became popular, Johnlone was one of the few domestic premium brands. For this first Chinese designer, one of the weekly musts was clothes shopping, and he went to Europe, Hong Kong and America once a year. He must have enough clothes to guarantee that he did not have to wear the same piece twice. In order to be different, he even made clothes by himself and he was fond of substituting the antique buttons he found in the overseas antique markets for those on the clothes he bought. He got a lot pleasure in these things which others might find troublesome and meaningless. He was completely absorbed in his paranoid aesthetics. When buying clothes, he never looked at the brand. It is said that this could increase the distinguishing capability and decrease the chance of inappropriate dressing. “Up to now, I have never dressed the same with others.”

1996年移民美国后他在欧洲到处旅行，回国后发现华人在设计方面有成就的很少，在国际设计领域没有地位，他便开始从事室内设计。“衣服是面料做的，你只是在跟布打交道。餐厅和酒吧听起来只是一个吃饭喝酒的消遣地方，其实它是一个很好的创作平台，可以营造不同的空间，肆意挥霍我设计和创作的欲望，也可以让我的收藏品物尽其用”。当汪兴政无法从服装设计中找到更多的乐趣与兴奋点，这样的转变是自然而然的。

In 1996 he immigrated to America and then toured around the Europe. Discovering that the Chinese designing had got no place at all in the international sphere, he began his career in interior designing. “Clothes are made of cloth and cloth is the only thing that engages your mind. Restaurant and bar sound like just a place for eating, drinking and entertaining. In fact it is a good platform which can give full play to my potentiality in design and creation and which can make the best use of my collection.” This turning from fashion to interior designing could not be more natural when he could no longer find satisfaction and excitement in the former.

1996年他创办第一家经营传统菜式的“鲜墙房”餐厅，带领“尊龙”服装设计团队全员转向鲜墙房的菜品设计，于是设计师成了导演，而厨师则变成了演员。“从菜的搭配、造型以及器皿的选择、环境的搭配，我认为与我做服装设计是相通的。”汪兴政认为，这些独特的元素构成了他理想中的餐厅：首先应该是美的。他创新地在餐饮行业引入文化、艺术元素，营业之初即成为上海有名的需要排队就餐的场所。直至今日，“鲜墙房”的每一个连锁店里的菜品、环境，在上海的高档餐馆中依然不落下风。2001年创办了将中西文化风格兼容并蓄的西餐厅和音乐酒吧“乾门（The Door）”，已成上海经典。同年，他开始投资并设计雍福会。

In 1996 he started Xian Qiangfang restaurant, the first one dealing in traditional dishes. He turned his Johnlone design team from the fashion design to the cuisine design, the designer becoming the director and the chefs the actors. “Personally I think fashion design has got a lot in common with food allocations, food shape, the choice of the vessel and the match with the surrounding.” Wang believed that these elements constituted his ideal restaurant: first and foremost, it should be beautiful. He creatively ushered cultural and artistic elements in the catering industry. At the very beginning of the business, his restaurant had become so popular that people had to wait in queue. Even today every restaurant in his Xian Qiangfang chain is still among the top as far as the cuisine and environment are concerned. In 2001 he founded “The Door”, a western restaurant and music bar that assimilated the west and the east elements. It is in the same year that he invested in and designed Yongfoo Elite.

将中国悠久文化底蕴以“美术”这种国际语言进行传达是汪兴政最得意之举，他把自己对服装的深刻理解带入整个园林的设计之中，因而使许多建筑细节都充满了人性化色彩。这位原籍上海、非建筑专业出身的服装设计师，骨子里有特别传统的东西，他非常喜欢那些小时候家里用过的老式家具，业余兴趣是逛世界各地的旧货和古董市场，收藏各种老东西。当他第一次在旧货市场上看见一张旧梳妆台，便立刻迷上了它。此后，便一发不可收拾。

Wang Xingzheng is good at conveying Chinese culture through fine arts, the international language. He brought his understanding of fashion into the garden design, rendering a lot of details in the building more humane. This Shanghai local fashion designer-turned architect has got something pretty traditional in him and he harbored a feeling for those old furniture he used to enjoy as a kid. Thus he developed a hobby of roaming through the second-hand markets and antique

雍福会一角
a corner of Yongfoo Elite

markets all over the world and collected all kinds of old stuff. When he for the first time caught sight of an old dressing table in a second-hand market, he fell in love with it at once. From then on nothing could hold him back at all.

他喜欢时间里的记忆痕迹，几十年来，一路走一路收，从中式家具到西式餐具，从雕花大床到丝绸沙发——只要是看见喜欢的，他都会买下来。直至小仓库放不下，换成大仓库，再到现在用来“陈列”这些收藏品的雍福会。最痴迷的时候，曾经三更半夜还在街上打着手电翻淘宝贝。汪兴政每年有一半时间在国外游历：伦敦、巴黎、罗马、巴塞罗那，他近乎狂热地追踪各种古玩市场和跳蚤市场的信息。英国诺丁汉有全世界最大的古董市场，绵延10英里，汪兴政一头栽进去，经常“负债”而归。在巴黎当地的圣·图安跳蚤市场里兜兜转转，那里有2,500个摊位，虽说货色质量参差不齐，不过值得人花时间精挑细选，他每次都能在那里待上一天，为的就是慧眼识珠的惊喜。

For dozens of years, he kept increasing his collection, from the Chinese furniture to the Western tableware, from carving bed to silk sofa. He would buy whatever that he loved. The warehouse for his collection was changed from a small one into a large one and finally Yongfoo Elite became the place where his antiques are on display. For some time he was so obsessed that he was seen looking for antiques in the midnight with a flashlight. Every year he spent half a year in travelling abroad: London, Paris, Rome, and Barce-lona, passionately keeping up with the information about the antique markets and second-hand markets. Nottingham in Britain has the largest antique market in the world that extends 10 miles, and Wang Xingzheng often returned from there, deep in debt. Saint-Ouen Flea Market in Paris was a worthwhile place to go with its 2500 stalls of various goods. He could roam there from morning till evening just for an item of surprise.

“设计师如果把古董里的美都领略一遍的话，境界一下子就能获得飞跃。”可以说，乾门和雍福会就是为他的宝贝们找一个表演的舞台。其中雍

❧石榴花开
pomegranate flowers in blossom

❧开阔的花园式庭院
the garden courtyard

福会陈列的大小近千件艺术精品及古董，均出自汪先生十数年的个人私藏，投入三千多万。

“If a designer can get to know and appreciate the beauty in the antiques, his capability can be enhanced greatly”. It is true that The Door and Yongfoo Elite are exactly the stage he finds for his collection. In Yongfoo Elite alone there are altogether a thousand pieces on display, all coming from Wang’s private collection with a worth of over 30 million Yuan.

雍福会的周围都是些高宅大院。夜晚来到此处，别有一番情趣。灯光昏暗、树影婆娑的小巷深处，梧桐树在橘黄色的灯光投影下格外漂亮。小巷、梧桐、路灯、飞蛾，行人零落，庭院深深的“雍福会”光影绰绰，透着一股宁静、神秘的气息。曲径通幽之后却豁然开朗，几盏温黄的灯火幽幽点亮了楼房里的云衣鬓影和园子里的名贵老树。庭院似乎未经打理，然而仔细一看，一切都布局讲究。

Yongfoo Elite is surrounded by mansions and courtyards. When darkness falls, it is a different view here. The plane trees and the alleys, bathed in the dim orange light, are unrealistically beautiful. Yongfoo Elite, set in the background of the lanes, the plane trees, the lamps, the moths and the occasional pedestrians, assumes some sense of mystery. However, the dim lamp betrays the genteel in the house and the rare trees in the yard. At first look, the yard seems neglected. Yet a second look might tell that all is in a perfect order.

门是一扇古色古香的小门。无论什么时候过去，门口总有三四个穿着深色西服、拿着对讲机的男人，有一点国宾馆的味道。车停过去，就有西服男人过来拉开门，并顺手接过车钥匙去泊到周围的公用停车库了。其他人先是轻声致以问候，而后带领着客人走进院子，曲折蜿蜒，登堂入室。毕竟是私人会所，服务非常到位、讲究。服务生也善解人意，有问必答，招之即来。

The door is quite quaint. Whenever you walk in, you can never fail to see three or four men in suit with interphones in hand, making it more like a state guesthouse. With the car pulling in, a man in suit will come over and help to park the car in the public parking lot nearby. The others will greet you and lead you through the winding yard to the club itself. After all it is a private club, with the service being the first class. The waiters are quite considerate and are always ready to answer your questions and serve you.

走进大门，你就置身于一条有四五米高的绿色植物夹成的甬道里，在高大的植物墙中，很有创意地用各色布镶嵌着。转过一个弯，远处似乎还有一张床，这多少令人感到是一种交错时光。若是春秋两季去那里，最普通的照片也能拍出挡不住的贵族气。

Walking inside, you find yourself in an aisle with green plants as high as four or five meters on both sides. And cloth of varieties of colors is dotted in these plant walls in a very creative way. Could be dimly viewed far away if you make a turn, which might make you feel lost in time. In spring and autumn, even a common picture can capture the unavoidable sense of nobility.

一个不经意，就会和某个女明星从二小姐的雕花大床边擦身而过，那边厢某个上市公司CEO可能在回廊里来回闲庭信步整理着思绪，而各国的领事和外交官们，则在包房里细细挑一根鱼骨头，听着梨花带雨从一面湖水飘过来的隐约扬琴声。

Here you might unconsciously brush past some female stars besides the carved bed; in the corridor a CEO of some listed company might be walking back and forth, lost in his own thoughts. And in some private rooms the consuls and the diplomats are enjoying the dishes, with the faintly dulcimer in their ears coming far from the lake.

雍福会走的是私人会所路线，内有上海餐馆、酒吧和只对会员开放的VIP房。是IAC（International Associate Clubs国际俱乐部联盟）在中国国内屈指可数的联盟会所之一。雍福会会员有权享用全球一百三十多家顶级私人会所，这对于会员的商务活动来说价值非凡，会员只需通过雍福会的转介，便可获得IAC成员俱乐部的会员接待礼遇，而无需加入当地国籍，即时进入到访国家主流社会，为会员的商务活动构筑了有效的交流平台。IAC在世界各地的私人会所不仅为会员提供了典雅舒适的环境和尽善尽美的私人化服务，更使会员无论到世界各地都有归家的感觉。

Yongfoo Elite, as a private club, has a Shanghai-style restaurant, bar and a VIP rooms for members only. It is one of the few members of IAC in China.

❧雍福会的白玉兰树
the magnolia tree in Yongfoo Elite

The members of Yongfoo Elite are entitled to the 130 top private clubs throughout the world, which proves to be very valuable for the business activities of the members. The members, through the referral of Yongfoo Elite, are entitled to the membership treatment in other IAC clubs. In this way, the members can get into the upper class in the visiting nation without being their citizens and it constitutes an effective platform for the commercial activities of the members. The private clubs attached to IAC not only provide a cozy and elegant environment as well as a perfect service but also give them a sense of belonging wherever they go.

百年“上海真滋味”
A Century of Shanghai Cuisine

自2004年开业以来，雍福会成功地吸引了商界精英，驻沪外国政府官员和社会名流加入其会员行列，成为中国一流商业场所的代表之一。话说“食、色，性也”，由于服务对象大都是时尚人士、社会名流，雍福会自然要对吃喝艺术有相当的研究。雍福会设计建造花了3年，试菜也用了3年，构思的结果是一个多元的、丰富的、跨度很大的组合体。什么样的菜能匹配这样的环境？选择西餐很容易，找个顶级大厨就好了。但是雍福会并没有采用西餐来搭配这里的环境，而是选择了中餐。

Since it started business in 2004, Yongfoo Elite has attracted foreign officials as well as celebrities as its members, thus becoming the representative of first-class commercial space in China. Confucius once said to the effect that the desire for food and sex is part of human nature. Since the members are mostly the social celebrities, they should be pretty particular about eating. Yongfoo Elite spent three years in exterior and interior design and cuisine design, the result of which is a diverse and rich complex. But what kind of cuisine can match the surrounding? The Western food is easy and a good chef is enough. Yet they did not employ the Western cuisine, instead they decide upon Chinese cuisine.

雍福会的中餐吸收了很多西方的做法，“我们用中国和西方两种思维方式对菜式进行了改良，让中国菜与雍福会的环境相容。比如有机蔬菜做的沙拉，我却在里头放了中式酱料和日式芥末，味道很特别。这就是雍福会在菜肴上的中西合璧”。这里能带给客人不一样的中西合璧的美食。

In Yongfoo Elite, they make the Chinese food in the Western way, “We innovate the cuisine by combining the Chinese and Western thinking modes, thus making the Chinese food in harmony with the environment in Yongfoo Elite. For instance, the vegetable salads with Chinese sauce and Japanese mustard taste very special. This is what we mean by saying we combine the West and the East in cuisine.”

上海人爱吃，会吃，懂得生活，传说上海菜里有一个现代人不大记起的单词：精致。很多来雍福会的人都是冲着“吃”来的。经典上海菜，就是老法做的上海菜，也叫“传菜”、本帮菜。老上海人都知道20世纪初，本帮菜最有名的大师傅叫李伯荣。雍福会的总厨丁永强先生掌勺三十余年，高级烹调技师，中国烹饪大师，更是一代“厨神”李伯荣的弟子，在来到雍福会以前，他曾是华亭宾馆的总厨，深谙本帮菜的精髓，并兼研川、扬、粤等菜系。可见这里本帮菜实力雄厚，淋漓尽致地透出了地地道道的百年“上海真滋味”。

Shanghainese love life and food. Exquisite is enough a word to describe the classic Shanghai cuisine. Not a few people come to Yongfoo Elite for the sake of food. The classic Shanghai cuisine, namely the cuisine made in the traditional way, is also called Benbang cuisine. It is well known in Shanghai that the master of Benbang cuisine in the beginning of 20th century was Li Borong. Ding Yongqiang, the head chef of Yongfoo Elite with the reputation as the Chinese Master Chef, is exactly the disciple of Li Borong, the gusteau. Before coming to Yongfoo Elite, he served as the head chef of Hua Ting Hotel and knew well the essence of Ben Bang cuisine and also studied Sichuan, Yangzhou and Cantonese cuisine. Thus here in Yongfoo Elite the chefs, deep-rooted in Benbang culture, are able to provide the gourmet with the absolute Shanghai flavor.

一百多年来，本帮菜海纳百川，兼容了徽菜的浓油赤酱、粤菜的精致清鲜、鲁菜的考究大气等“八大菜系，十六帮别”的“秘诀”，经本地化改良后，形成了以“雅”见长，底蕴深厚，被称为颇有“文人情怀”的本帮特色。如今，“选料精细，讲究火功，粗细兼长，四季分明”的本帮菜更重天然、健康、绿色，严把进料关、拒绝添加剂，在“营养食补，味道多元”上研发创新。

For more than a hundred years, Ben Bang cuisine has assimilated the essence of other cuisines, such as the abundance of oil and sauce of Anhui cuisine, the freshness of Guangdong cuisine and elegance of Shandong cuisine. After innovation, Benbang cuisine is characterized by elegance. Today Benbang cuisine, particular about material and cooking process, gives more heed to the natural, healthy and green diet. It is strict about the material and refuses the use of any additives, trying to come up with nutritious and diversified cuisine.

本帮菜的酱油十分讲究，几乎能决定一道菜品的好坏。雍福会的酱油是秘制的，有独家秘方，概不外传。在这里一群最有名的厨师，自己酿造酱油，因为只有原汁原味的酱油，才能制作出酱鸭、酱鸡等多种酱菜组合的雍福会的招牌菜——“酱拼”，才能做出最正宗的上海菜。所谓酱拼，就是有酱鸭、河虾、瑶柱和白果做成的拼盘，再配上青葡萄点缀。绿色葡萄下的干冰，散发缕缕轻烟，淡化了浓油赤酱在色泽上的单调。它似曾相识，仿佛昔日妈妈每年用酱油浸的菜，酱拼以前其实就是上海人吃早饭时的菜。酱拼里用的瑶柱必须一般大小，规格统一，要经过严格筛选。

Benbang cuisine is very fastidious about soy sauce, which could be the key of a dish. The soy sauce used in Yongfoo Elite is made by themselves with the recipe kept in secret. Generally speaking, the chefs brew soy sauce by themselves, because only with specially made soy sauce, can they finish the specialty in Yongfoo Elite, the Jiangpin （marinated meat combination in soy sauce）. The so-called Jiangpin is a dish of sauced duck, shrimp, scallops and ginkgo, with green grapes in the middle of the plate. When water is pumped in the dry ice under the grapes, thin smoke rises up to render the color less monotonous. The dish can easily remind the Shanghainese of the breakfast mother used to prepare. The scallops in the dish must be of the same size and strictly chosen.

拌生鱼，用花生酱、芥末、少量醋拌好生的海鲈鱼丝，以红萝卜衬底，原来上海菜也可以这样好看。

The Raw Fish in Sauce is a dish with the bass mixed with peanut butter, mustard, some vinegar and carrots. Actually Benbang cuisine can be as beautiful as it is tasteful.

同样浓油赤酱的油爆河虾，完全遵照“甜上口，咸收口”师训办事。做这道菜时，厨工把虾脚剪掉，让壳肉分离，再把油烧至9成热，放入备好的河虾，虾在锅里只有二十几秒的时间而已，这样就保证了虾肉的鲜嫩。不甜不咸的口味保证了它不会有收口时的苦味。而油爆虾也同酱拼里的瑶柱一样，都是一般大小，这样的精益求精，值得敬佩。

Fried River Shrimp, equally heavy in oil and sauce, tastes sweet at first and then a little salty. When cooking this dish, the chef fries the shrimps, with the feet cut off and the shell peeled off, in the hot oil for only about 20 seconds to guarantee the freshness of the shrimps. The dish is neither too sweet nor too salty, which prevents the bitter taste. The shrimps, just like the scallops in the Jiangpin, are of the same size.

本帮菜的核心就在于蟹。蟹粉豆腐，蟹必须是最佳时节的，而在“九雌十雄”的“蟹季”，现拆蟹粉蟹黄，一点不含糊，可以各归各，都好吃。而如今合在一起，更和谐，更美味。

The key to Benbang cuisine is the crabs, Beancurd with Hairy Crab Meat is one of such dishes. The crabs must be right in season when they are pretty fat. The crab meat and the crab cream, delicately separated, can be pretty tasty. When cooked as a whole, the crab is even more delicious and appealing.

清炒手剥河虾仁，拣得一般大小的河虾仁，虾仁自然是一个个人工剥出的，没冻过，味道自然不凡；“草头圈子”里的草头选的是精华；特别要讲讲火腿炖老母鸡，先是用老母鸡熬了浓浓的汤，鸡肉弃之不食。再取另一只鸡，用这浓鸡汤炖，加上以火腿增味，用竹荪让牙齿舒适地多磨几下，酽酽一碗下肚，若是深秋时节，头上汗珠也细细沁出，可以说是过瘾，更会让人觉得，吃到好东西真是世间少有的快事。哪怕是简简单单一碗绿豆汤的做法，也是先蒸、加糖、再蒸的做法，远远区别于自己家里加水一煮了之的粗糙。蔬果则选用青木瓜、牛油果之类的西式原料，却由酱油调制而成，是地道的西餐中吃，甜咸相配；同样，做枣泥酥饼的枣泥馅也是买来枣子自己磨出来的，这恰是《红楼梦》里才有的精致生活。

Sauteed Fresh Water Shrimp is another specialty in Yongfoo. The fresh shrimps, of the same size and with the shells peeled off by the chefs. Another dish is Cao Tou Quan Zi, which is a dish with intestine and clover, with the latter well-chosen. The next one is the Stewed Hen. First the chef uses a hen to make the soup, then he takes another hen and stews it in the soup together with sausage and bamboo shoots. On a winter day a bowl of such soup can immediately warm you up and make you feel that eating can be such great fun in the world. Even Green Bean Soup, which is so common in our household, is made so delicate and exquisite here in Yongfoo Elite. As for the vegetables and fruits, Yongfoo Elite tend to choose the Western material, such as green papaya and avocado, and make them in traditional Chinese way. Likewise, when the chefs make Crispy Dates Mud Pancake, they prefer to buy the dates and grind them. It is exactly the kind of life as is described in Dream in the Red Mansion.

这里实行套餐制，客人不需要点菜，只需预订座位和消费标准就好，厨师自会根据季节与时令寻找特别的用料确定当日的菜品与甜品，全部选用最新鲜、最天然的原材料烹制。上海菜本身四季分明，是典型的“节气菜”，但凡素菜，就应当在当令的时候吃，比如春笋、韭菜等。孔夫子也曾说过“不时不食”，就是这个道理。做“节气菜”，本身也是对中国的饮食文化的传承。

In Yongfoo Elite guests only need to reserve the seats and set a standard for the consumption, and the chef will decide upon the dish and the desert according to the season to make sure that everything is fresh and natural. Benbang cuisine is a seasonal cuisine with all the vegetables right in season. Confucius once said, “Eat only those in season”. Benbang cuisine in itself is a heritage of the Chinese catering culture.

菜有“菜性”，原料与原料在烹饪过程中互相补充，从而凸显出这道菜的品质，大厨的能力就显现在能否发现菜性上。这里的菜式融入了古法烹调，使用自制酱料，口味较清淡，再加上中餐西吃的新颖模式，使得古典上海菜颇有旧貌换新颜的意境，既体现了海派文化的宽容与精致，菜式的精美设计又为时尚赋予了经典内涵。品的是本帮地道口味，享的是精准西式服务，重拾的是十里洋场的典雅生活品位。

Each dish has its own feature. Different materials, in the process of cooking, complement each other and make the dish special. The chef is the very person who is capable of discovering the feature of a dish. The dishes here in Yongfoo Elite, cooked in the traditional way with the secretly brewed sauce, take on some novelty when they are served in the Western way. Specially designed dishes not only embody the tolerance of Shanghai culture but endow fashion with special meaning. It is here that you are actually eating local cuisine while enjoying typical

Western service and it is here that life in old Shanghai is a dream come true.

无法穿越的旧式浮华
The Irreversible Luxury of the Past

对大多数的客人而言，吃经典的上海菜并不是他们到雍福会的唯一目的。无论什么时候，主人汪兴政的目的只有一个，就是让每一位到雍福会的客人心情

❧ 雍福会二楼回廊
the corridor on the second floor

放松，享受生活的惬意，“我做雍福会和餐饮没什么关系，只想通过一个平易近人的平台和客人交流。客人在这里得到的将是意料不到的惊喜和经验。”——最初他自己都没有把握，如何将东方情调与西方审美融合，最后却颠覆了和谐，所有物件与藏品越过时空界限比肩而邻：可以肆意地躺在清代的鸦片床上把酒贪欢；可以到以“菜香书屋”命名的酒吧中小憩；还可以坐在完全西式的银餐具中间细细把玩清代那些匪夷所思的三寸绣花鞋；更可以暗自品味隐喻着贾宝玉为林黛玉的伤逝而悲泣的，意寓“千红一哭”的红木大门……一树、一花、一灯，地上的瓷砖，墙上风格迥异的镜子，留有上任主人回忆的旧桌布，都经过了精心挑选，不动声色地喧哗着。

For most guests, the Benbang cuisine is not their only aim in Yongfoo Elite. Wang Xingzheng, the host, has always adhered to one purpose, that is, to give the guest a chance to relax and enjoy life. “What I do in Yongfoo has got nothing to do with catering industry. It is just a platform to communicate with the guests. The guests will have a surprise and a special experience when they get here”. At first he was not sure how to mix the West and the East, yet finally he subverted the harmony and all the items, old and new, Eastern and Western, coexist here regardless of time and space. Here you can just lie on the opium bed from Qing Dynasty with a drink; here you can rest a bit in the bar named “Savoury Study”; here you can appreciate the three-inch embroidered shoes in Qing Dynasty sitting among the Western silver wares; here you can come to the red wood door to pay tribute to the love between Jia Baoyu and Lin Daiyu; here, everything, from the tree to the lamp, from the mirror to the old cloth, is well-chosen and tells its own story.

可以说，雍福会是上海近百年历史变迁中，西洋文化和中国古文化的天作之合，如同贝多芬的G大调般在冲突的旋律中体现出和谐的美感，仿佛穿越多个时空的杰作，而这又绝非刻意的复辟。正是这种深刻的文化魅力，深深吸引了法国前总统夫人贝尔纳黛特·希拉克、NBA球星姚明、香港商界名流关裕彤、李泽楷、巨星成龙等名人，成为名流圈的宠儿。

Yongfoo Elite is a marriage between the West and the Chinese cultures. Just as Beethoven’s G major that creates harmony out of conflicts, Yongfoo Elite mixes the conflicting cultures in one. It is this cultural charm that attracts the attentions and remains the favorite of all kinds of social celebrities, such as the former French first lady Bernadette Chirac, NBA superstar Yao Ming and Jackie Chan the movie star.

在雍福会的大门口，几乎看不到任何景致，两侧看似随意栽种的松柏和冬青，曲曲折折有如屏障，把院内景致遮得严严实实，也遮住了所有向里张望的眼睛，私密性极强。据说在雍福会，树的栽种要看属性，一草一木均渗透着古今、东西各异的文化气质。

At the entrance of Yongfoo Elite, there is nothing except the pines and hollies on both sides, concealing everything within. It is said that in Yongfoo Elite even the trees are well-chosen, showing the distinction between the two cultures.

穿过锈迹斑斑的绿色铁栅门，沿着小径走进去，并不显眼的红墙灰瓦毫不招摇，墙上写着不大不小的“雍福会”三个字和“The Yongfoo Elite”的英文名，正楷字与英文摆在一起，已经在告诉访客，这是个中西合璧的场所。下方的浮雕是中国古代常出现的“蝙蝠莲花图”，“蝠”与“福”同音，因此蝙蝠在中国文化中被认为是幸福的象征；而莲花也是传统的吉祥图案。大门旁边还有块充满老上海风情的招牌迎风招展。还未进门，低调、古典与时尚的奢华感已经迎面扑来。

Going through the rusty green door and walking on along the path, you come to the wall with the Yongfoo Elite writen in both English and Chinese. The Chinese and the English standing together tell visitors already that this is a place of both the West and the East. The relief below is the traditional Chinese "bat and lotus graph". In Chinese bat and blessing are pronounced the same, as a result, bat is considered the symbol of happiness in Chinese culture; lotus is traditionally an auspicious pattern. Beside the door a signboard typical of old Shanghai is swinging in the breeze. You are confronted with some classic and fashionable sense of luxury before you actually get inside.

甬道的尽头豁然开朗处，便是旁边那座看起来并不张扬的会所主楼。小小的入口依旧低调，像是到了旧上海某大户人家的公馆。在这样的外国建筑的门楣上，居然挂了一幅中国的匾额，上书“聚德堂”三个字，意为“德才兼备，德在先”那么贴切，合情合理。

At the end of the aisle stands the modest main building of the club. The small entrance is exactly like that to the mansion of some rich families in old Shanghai. On the lintel of such a Western-style building, there hangs a Chinese plaque with three characters of Ju De Tang, meaning virtue comes before talent. All seems so proper and reasonable.

推门而入，湖蓝色的雕花墙布与上方的铜制西式顶灯发出的黄色光晕让这个不大的门厅充满奢华的味道。门厅左边有一个典型的西洋壁炉，壁炉上方则是匾额，上面是乾隆年间刘墉的题刻真迹“履无咎盦（庵）”，意为放松一下，自由自在，字苍劲清俊。匾下放着清乾隆十七年吉日造的香炉。有趣的是，它的外形有点像现代浴缸。壁炉前，安置着一个大圆桌，这是让等座的客人休息的，黑漆剥落的圆桌，黑漆剥落的椅子，在幽暗的光线下试图还原古老的日子。在这里落座，和刘墉的用意恰恰相反，你会体验到大户人家拘谨的时光。

When you push the door open and walk in, the lake-blue wallpaper and the dim

雍福会主楼聚德堂
Ju De Tang, the main building in Yongfoo Elite

yellow light from the Western-style ceiling lamp overhead fill the small hall with luxury. On the left side of the hall is a typical western mantel piece and above the fireplace is a plaque written by Liu Yong himself in Qing Dynasty to the effect of relaxation and freedom. Under the plaque is a thurible built in the 17th year during Qian Long's reign, which resembles the modern tub. In front of the fireplace, there is a round table for the waiting guests. In the dim light the table and the chairs, with the paint gone, seem to try to restore the old days. Sitting here, instead of relaxing as Liu Yong's plaque suggests, you will feel reserved.

经过西式吧台，转向左边，就到了一楼的主用餐区域。面积并不大的用餐区采用金黄色的墙布，10张餐桌前摆放着各种古典款式的欧式座椅或卧榻，很西式的感觉。靠窗的位置临着连廊，墙边有一长案，上面有几只老皮箱，透明银色藤蔓花纹的玻璃瓶中插着一大束白色的香水百合，香气淡淡。

Walking past the bar counter and turning left, you will come to the catering area on the first floor. Small-sized, the area is quite Western with the golden wallpaper and the varieties of chairs or couches put around the 10 tables. The seats beside the window are next to the corridor and there is a long table with several old leather cases. A large bouquet of white lilies in a glass bottle sends out faint fragrance.

银色方盘托白色餐盘，白色手工绣台布，窗幔十分特别，蓝色的横着垂下，红色上绣孔雀尾羽。旧式橱柜里摆放的古董都是主人的收藏。一副对联“东鲁雅言诗书达礼；西京明训孝弟力田”挂在大厅中央，却不显突兀。不仔细看，很难发现原来这是用玻璃烧制出来的精仿匾额。说到匾额的精细程度，举个例子，就连行书间的细小连笔都保持完好，一根也没有断开。黑色老式钢琴，绿色的织花帘幔，顶上的多头吊灯也穿着同色的织花外衣。大厅是铜制的顶，斜对面墙的一小半是镶着各色玻璃的门，一面挂着中式的中堂画和对联。

Everything here is dreamlike, such as the silver tray, the white plates, the white cloth with hand embroidery. The curtain is pretty special, with the blue one drawn and peacock feathers embodied in the red one. The old cupboards stored the collections of the owner. A couplet is hanging right in the middle of the hall, strange yet harmonious. Only when examining it carefully can you discover it is a glass plaque. It is so exquisite that even the tiniest detail is well preserved at all. And there stands an old black piano with the green broche curtain and even the pendent lamps wear the same broche clothes. The ceiling of the hall is made of copper. On one side of the wall is a stained-glass door and on another wall are the paintings and Chinese couplets.

用餐区包括一楼主厅、一楼两个包房和紧邻庭院的户外露台，二楼是中厅、小厅、两个包房和会员专用的阳光屋，以及三楼一个包房。虽然是典型的复古西洋建筑，但是漫步其中，却会以为置身于一个古老传统的中国大家族的宅院。这里汇聚了太多的中国审美，有着无法穿透的旧式浮华。

The catering area includes a hall, two private rooms on the first floor and the outdoors balcony adjoining the courtyard. On second floor are the big hall, the small hall, two private rooms and a sunshine room for the members only. There is another private room on the third floor. Though a classic western building, it makes you feel present in a traditional Chinese mansion. Here there are too many elements concerning the beauty and luxury in old Shanghai.

再穿过一段玻璃回廊，眼前是一座七分中国风加上三分西洋气的庭院。步入这个中国式庭院，只几步就是一面很显眼的深色花岗岩砌成的墙，不细看根本发现不了那扇门，门楣上方一幅大匾嵌在墙里，上书三字“密训堂”，明晃晃得发亮。据说此处原为大户人家父亲教诲子女之处，是“不与外人语”的地方。然而这里现在却已经换上一扇完全现代化的红外线电控自动门。门旁边有一副对联，“数世士农承祖德，千秋羹酤来思成”，大意就是几代日子都是靠祖先辛苦积累而成。

Going through a section of glass corridor, you come to a courtyard that is a mixture of the Chinese and the Western styles. Several steps in this Chinese courtyard will bring in view a granite wall in dark colour, in which the door is hardly discernible. On the lintel is a plaque deeply embedded in the wall with three shining Chinese characters “Mi Xun Tang”. It is said that here is the place where the father in the rich family delivered instructions to his children, therefore, it is a place kept in secret. But today the door has been replaced by a modern automatic one with electric control. Beside the door is a couplet to the effect that this life has been possible because of the hard work of successive generations.

走进去，紧挨着门的左首是摆放祭祀用品的地方，现在则依着形迹很巧妙地变成了酒吧的吧台。沿着窄窄的酒吧过去，维多利亚时代的椭圆镜和中国古代的供堂相对而立；旁边西式的贵妃塌静静地挨在中式雕花窗边；在中国古代的雕花大门上，镶嵌的西洋的彩色玻璃，阳光射进来，就融化了太平洋。那座20世纪60年代初生产的英国第一代冰箱静静地驻守在后门口，宽阔的把手像现在的汽车门把手，据说除了声音有点大，其他运转还一切正常。

Inside in door, on the left, which used to be the place for sacrifice, now stands a bar counter. Moving through the narrow bar, you will see the Victorian oval mirror and the Chinese consecrate hall standing face to face; a Western chaise longue is lying quietly near the Chinese carved window; on the Chinese carved door are the colorful Western stained glass, which seems intoxicating in the sunshine. The refrigerator produced in England in 1960s stand at the back door, with the large handle more like that on a car. It is said that it works well except the loud noise.

密训堂其实是酒吧，酒类很是丰富，鸡尾酒多达数十种，有雍福会的特制鸡尾酒（dry martini），另有开胃酒、金酒、伏特加、朗姆酒、龙舌兰酒等。白酒、黄酒也应有尽有。吧台上有20世纪30年代大美烟公司招牌和20世纪50～60年代的电话机。这个酒吧里摆放着各式仿古的家具，特意做了仿古处理的镜子，旧痕斑驳。玻璃的天顶，客人可坐在里面晒晒太阳，品着下午茶。握一杯酒置身其中，恍惚已进入了一个大家族的神秘历史。

Mi Xun Tang is actually a bar with a variety of liquor provided, including dry martini, rum, vodka and tequila. On the counter is a telephone in the 1960s. All kinds of replicas of antique furniture are placed in the bar to go with the environment. With a glass ceiling overhead, the guests can sit and, enjoy the sunshine and the afternoon tea. With a wine glass in hand, you feel like you have entered the history of a mysterious family.

菜香书屋，名字有点俗，可能主人想大俗即大雅吧。它偏安在院子的一角，是雪茄吧，石头雕花门洞，玻璃的自动门，清代的门挡，门口悬挂着一个匾额，上书“悬规”二字，门内的匾额则写着“植矩”二字，“悬规植矩”可以让我们想起中国的古话“循规蹈矩”，但其实是完全相反的概念。“循规蹈矩”是守规，“悬规植矩”是立规。前一个代表的是守法者的信条，后一个则代表的是立法者的做法。“我不用规矩的手法去设计雍福会，但做出来的东西又是规矩的，所以叫‘植矩’。”

Savoury Study is a cigar bar situated at a corner of the yard with the stone door opening and the door shield from Qing Dynasty. A plaque is hanging at the door, saying “Xuan Gui” and another plaque hanging inside saying “Zhi Ju”. The two plaques remind us of a Chinese saying,”Xun Gui Dao Ju” which means that we should obey the rules. But in fact the plaques here “Xuan Gui Zhi Ju” means something totally opposite, that is, we should set up rules. The former refers to the belief of the ruled and the latter the belief of the rulers. Just as Wang Xingzheng said, “I did not intend to design Yongfoo Elite out of the usual mode, yet the finally designed Yongfoo Elite is rule-abiding, hence ‘Zhi Ju’.”

那里最著名的是绿色的1960年生产的古驰沙发，历经近五十年的时光流逝，它却依然完好。成龙、张曼玉每次到这里，是一定要来坐一回的。据说某次，古驰的总裁到上海，看到这套绿色的沙发也不禁感慨万千。与之相对应的是明代的太师椅和八仙桌，上面铺着清代的金绣，正中间绣着一个“寿”字。围绕“寿”字绣了5只象征着福气的蝙蝠，最外面则绣着8种不同的器皿，借指传说中的八仙，绣艺精湛。这张清代铺在大户人家桌子上的桌巾，隐含“寿字当先，五福临门，八仙过海，各显神通”之意。一个大家族的热闹和盛世好像都堆在这张桌子上了。不远处一张明代的富家千金小姐床占据在房间的一角，原木色很淡雅，红色的垂花，不像那些金碧辉煌的绣床，让人联想到窈窕淑女的闺房，顶上三分之一是透明的玻璃。就如地面，一段的青砖，几大片的明丽几何瓷砖，甚至还有亚克力的地面，木地板的老式拼纹中间亦要生生点缀上一小块西式碎花瓷砖，款款花式不同。东西方的结合，带来古今家私的视觉冲击，这般的中西合璧，简直美到了骨头里。壁炉上随意放着一幅印有溥仪肖像的皇帝牌香烟广告。墙上天花板上桌上，灯盏盏不同，柔和的灯光，幽暗的爵士乐，品酒聊天或点一支雪茄都很惬意。

The most eye-catching thing in this bar is the green Gucci couch made in 1960s. Fifty years of time has changed nothing about it. Jackie Chan and Maggie Chan would sit there every time they come. It is said that the president of Gucci once came to Shanghai, he could not control his emotion when seeing this green couch. Corresponding to the couch are the old-fashioned wooden armchairs and the square table with the gold embroidery on top. Right in the middle of the embroidery is a "Shou" meaning longevity, around which are 5 bats symbolizing blessing and 8 different kinds of vessels, referring to the eight immortals in the legend. This table cloth embodies longevity, great blessing and immortality.

The cloth itself says about the prime and prosperity of the traditional rich family. At a corner is a bed for the daughter of rich family. The bed is simple with red tassels, different from the gorgeous bed that reminds one of a boudoir. One third of the ceiling of the bar is transparent glass, just as the floor which is a combination of brick, ceramic tile and timber. The timber floor is dotted with a small piece of Western-style tile of various patterns. The combination of the West and the East brings a visual shock. On the fireplace is randomly placed an advertisement for Emperor Cigarettes with a portrait of Fu Yi, the last Chinese Emperor on it. The lights on the wall, the ceiling and the table are of different styles. The soft light and the Jazz music make drinking or smoking such a pleasant enjoyment here.

穿出木制的回廊，走到庭院南侧，便是这一片建筑里最令人叹为观止的、被题名为“六艺堂”的一段长廊。一面墙里镶嵌着一扇中式大门，门上方矗立着明代著名书法家杨逸书写的“六艺堂”三字书匾，指西周时的礼、乐、射、御、书、数六种技能。后来也指六经，即孔子编撰的《诗》、《书》、《礼》、《乐》、《易》、《春秋》。六艺堂即是展现才华的地方。

Walking through the wooden corridor and coming to the south of the courtyard, you will see the most amazing thing in this building, the long corridor named "Liu Yi Tang". A Chinese style door is set in the wall, above which is the plaque written by Yang Yi, the famous calligrapher in Ming Dynasty. On the plaque are the three Chinese characters "Liu Yi Tang", referring to the six skills, namely,

浓荫遮天的永福路
the shaded Yong Fu Road

music, archery, mathematics, ritual, chariot riding and calligraphy. They mean the same thing with what we call Six Books, that is, *Odes*, *History*, *Changes*, *Spring and Autumn*, *Rituals*, and *Music*. Therefore Liu Yi Tang is the place to show one's talent.

中央的红色大门原为某宗族祠堂之门，与长廊相配让人有推门观景之欲。门两侧有金色墙壁纹枝蔓图案，有大富大贵之相。屋顶上还特意为院子里那棵老柿子树留下一格空间。两边紧接着西藏风格的布墙。这些布墙是汪先生自己做的，先贴上整幅白布，然后再用油画颜料手绘上色，使之历久弥新，在上海的多雨气候中不会发霉。而作为一个开放的长廊，这里现在常用作表演，主要以戏曲为主。门两侧并放着一对明清时的木椅，甚至可以想像在某一个传统的家族仪式上，严父慈母端坐其上。边品尝美食，边享受中国戏曲，别有滋味。

The red door in the center used to be the door of a family ancestral hall. When set in the corridor, it invites people to push it open and see inside. On the both sides of the door are golden walls with the patterns of branches, meaning great prosperity. At the roof some space is spared for the old persimmon tree in the yard. Next to the golden walls are the cloth walls of Tibet style. These walls were made by Wang Xingzheng himself. First he glued the white cloth on the wall and then painted it with oil paint. As an open corridor, it serves as a stage for a lot of performances, especially opera. A pair of antique chairs are set on the both sides of the door. It can be imagined that at a traditional family ritual, the mother and the father sat here, enjoying delicacies as well as the opera.

六艺堂来自从江南完整迁移的清初木造宏伟大宅院厅堂，气势雄伟，廊檐精工细雕，人物景色栩栩如生。顶部的黄杨木雕上刻着许多知名历史场景，如三英战吕布等，人物鲜活逼真，是典型的中国式的精致。这段建于清朝的长廊，现在在以木刻最为著名的东阳也属罕见。先要将长廊像积木一样拆下来，每一个构件写上编号，花费了半年时间后，在上海重新组装完成。

Liu Yi Tang, as a whole, was moved here from the Changjiang Delta Area where this wooden hall was very typical in the beginning of Qing Dynasty, with the eaves finely carved. Some famous historical events are carved on the wood at the top and it is a typical example of Chinese art. Even in Dongyang which is well-known for its wood carving, this corridor is a rarity. Wang Xingzheng disassembled the corridor like building blocks and numbered each piece. And when he moved it to Shanghai, he spent half a year in rebuilding it.

在把六艺堂树立起来之后，它所带来的霸气让所有人束手无策，因为它与这里的环境太不相容了。封建时代的建筑特色是有思想的，有一股子帝王气。于是他们把它拆掉重来，前后一共拆了3次，每拆装一次就得付出数百万元的代价，但汪先生还是不满意。后来他想到，只有用更强的东西将它的帝王气息压住，才能改变突兀的感觉。“我想到西方皇室里的金碧辉煌，于是决定用两面金墙来压住它。具体办法就是把金箔贴在做过氧化处理的钢板上。六艺堂带来的是中国的帝王气息，金墙则代表了西方的帝王气息。但这样还是压不住。我又想到了宗教，宗教好比第三个帝王。于是才有了两边代表藏传佛教的花布墙。这三样放在一起，才达到平衡。这就好像上演了一出3位帝王的话剧。外国人来到这里，觉得很震撼，说我用的是‘上帝之手’。我说我用的元素是文化，是文化的力量”。

After it was set up, it appeared to be so domineering that it did not go well with the surrounding here. The building in the feudal age took a kind of kingly splendor with it. Therefore, it was dissembled and rebuilt for as many as three times, costing millions each time. Yet Wang Xingzheng was not satisfied. Finally it occurred to him that only something more imposing could possibly dominate it and make it less strange. “I thought about the royal palace in the west and decided upon the golden walls. Exactly speaking, it is to glue gold foil on the oxidated steel plates. Liu Yi Tang creates the Eastern kingly splendor and the golden walls the Western one. But it is far from enough. He thought about religion, which is just like the third king, hence the cloth walls on both sides that represent Tibetan Buddhism. When these three are put together, a balance is achieved. It is just like an opera about three kings. The foreigners are shocked at this, saying this is the hand of God. But he prefer to say it is the power of culture.

和这个区域所有花园洋房一样，雍福会三亩占地面积中，很大一部分是花园。现在，主人独出心裁地在花园沿围墙处以不同的表现手法造出了另一番天地。花园里摆放着古老的鸦片床，距“六艺堂”不远处矗立着一座石碑，源源不断的水流沿石碑表面缓缓滑入碑下的小潭里，潭边正对石碑摆着一个形状古朴的大缸，想来该是旧时灭火所用。最妙的是石碑正面上方凹形深处摆放着数盏烛台，水帘正从烛台外面飘飘而下，烛光透过水纹荧荧跳跃，本来“水火不容”，在这里却偏偏喻指“水能容火”。主人的意思是：天大的事情也要冷静，坐下来慢慢谈。紧挨着这个别致的“喷泉”，就放着几张闲散的桌椅，供客人们闲坐交流。

Just like the garden villas in this area, the majority of Yongfoo Elite, as much as 2000 square meters is occupied by garden. Now the owner just creates another world in the garden. The opium bed in the garden is one of the ideas. There is a stone tablet near Liu Yi Tang, and water runs non-stop along the tablet into the pool beneath. Beside the pool is a large vat which might be used to put out fire in the old days. The most striking is that several candlesticks are set in the concave of the table. With the water running in front, the dancing candle light is seen within. It is here that the traditional thought that water and fire are incompatible is totally reversed. Through this, the owner is trying to convey the idea that nothing cannot be dealt with as long as one remains calm. Beside this spring, several tables and chairs are set for the visitors.

可以说，这处庭院花园就是金木水火土的聚合：金——长廊墙壁上的金箔；木——庭院里的参天古木；水——鱼池；火——水帘后的烛火；土——庭院的草地。汪兴政刻意让这五个元素和谐地统一在一起，就是为了创造出五行生生相克的感觉。水帘后的烛火又引出了“水火相容”的概念，意思就是在雍福会，即便是最不和谐的元素也能相安无事。他将金、木、水、火、土各元素运用到极致的效果，营造出中西合璧、古典时尚、天人合一的独特感觉。“我希望通过一些比较现代的做法来表现这些有着精湛手艺，积淀了岁月美感的古旧东西，让客人使用它，了解它”。

This garden is a combination of the traditional five elements: gold, which can be found from the golden wall; wood, which is the trees in the yard; water as in the pool; fire as reflected by the candle behind the water; and soil as the grass land in the yard. Wang Xingzheng consciously put these five elements harmoniously together here to show that even the most conflicting elements can have a chance to become compatible in Yongfoo Elite. He used the five elements so perfectly that he created this special world where the West and the East, the classic and the fashion, the creature and the nature can coexist well. "I hope to present these beautiful and exquisite antiques through methods acceptable to the modern people, I want people to see them and know them", Wang said.

一场华美上海旧梦
A Dream of Old Shanghai

早在2001年，主人汪兴政信步游走至永福路200号英国领事馆旧址时，这处建筑因为无人问津，早已破败失修。当时英国领事馆的官员已经从这里迁出，此处便在空置的岁月中长满了荒芜。在汪兴政的手中，它被打扮得光鲜动人，重新打造了一个过去，向世界开放，把握的是那个年代特有的"当东方遇到西方"。大户人家客堂间里的牌匾、对联安在了新派人家里的欧式壁炉上，明代千金小姐的床和20世纪60年代的古驰沙发相安无事，印有毛泽东头像的陶瓷杯那么固执地和大红底色的英式茶杯放在一起。

As early as 2001, when Wang was walking to this former British Consulate, this building was forgotten and shabby. With the British officials long moved out, the place was taken over by weeds. Wang made her into a fair lady and presented her to the world. It is a place where the West meets the East. All the things here, radically different as they are, stay naturally with one another: the traditional plaque and couplet hang squarely on modern fireplace; the bed from Ming Dynasty stays peacefully with the Gucci couch in the 1960s; and the cup with the picture of Chairman Mao sits stubbornly next to the red British cup.

从商业角度来看，汪兴政承认自己是个糟糕的设计师，因为这个作品只让他拼命地花钱。"雍福会是我的梦想吧，我想做一件别人没做过的事情。如果说我在做这件事情的时候投入了很多的资金，那也只是我个人的享乐，我十分享受创建雍福会的那3年时间。我并没有把雍福会定位成一个要赚钱的投资，而是认为当中国经济发展到现在，在上海需要有这样一个东西，可

❧ 雍福会侧面
side of Yongfoo Elite

以从一个侧面代表这个城市，反映人们的生活状态，这些信息一定不是通过摩天大楼来体现的，我决定来做这样的一件事”。

Commercially speaking, Wang Xingzheng admits that he is a bad designer, because he spent so much on Yongfoo Elite. " Yongfoo Elite is my dream, I just want to do something unprecedented. I did invest a lot in it, yet I also enjoyed the process of establishing it. I did not found Yongfoo Elite for commercial purpose. I just believe that there should be a thing capable of reflecting the city and its people, which doesn't necessarily have to be a skyscraper. This is what I strive for.

为了实现这个目标，汪兴政心目中的“雍福会”几易其稿。按照汪兴政的原计划，雍福会的设计只用半年时间，但是“越做越过瘾”的汪兴政将设计足足拖了2年零8个月还意犹未尽。据说当年做雍福会的那些装修施工人员，最怕的就是汪老板盯住一个地方看超过5分钟以上，因为那就意味着，他又觉得哪个地方不对劲了，又要重新来过。“我想我是在用艺术家的头脑做一件商业的事情，如果我一直想着怎么取得商业回报，雍福会早就不存在了，那个创建的过程本身就是违背商业规律的。资金、时间、心血……所有投入都远超过传统运营的预算。即便现在你们看到的雍福会也不仅是一个商业空间，更多的是人文空间”。

To realize this dream, Wang Xingzheng changed his design time and time again. According to his plan, the design would be finished in half a year. Yet in fact Wang Xingzheng used actually as long as two years and eight months. It is said that the workers were afraid whenever Wang stared at a place for more than 5 minutes, because that would mean redoing the work. “I think I was doing something commercial with the mindset of an artist. If I had always thought about commercial rewarding, Yongfoo Elite would not have been here at all. The creation goes against the commercial rules. The time, the money and the energy have far surpassed the budget. Even now Yongfoo Elite you see is more a cultural place than a commercial one.”

经过反复修改，这里在2004年才建成营业。“每年房租和人工的成本要几百万元，如果以赚钱为目的，肯定不是这么做的，做第一家鲜墙房时我只用了36天，但是雍福会我用了三年”。“雍福会”也给了汪兴政一个意外，在开业两年后就已经实现盈利，无论是上海本地还是世界各地到上海的名流，“雍福会”都成为上海顶级消费场所的重要候选对象。

After constant alterations, it was finally completed and opened in 2004. “The annual rent and the human costs need millions of Yuan each year. I would not have done this if I had wanted to make money. I spent only thirty-six days in designing my first Xian Qiang Fang restaurant and three years in Yongfoo Elite.” Yet Yongfoo Elite in turn gave Wang Xingzheng a surprise. Only two years after Yongfoo Elite started business, it began to make profit. For the celebrities in Shanghai or other parts of the world, Yongfoo Elite is their top choice.

“做雍福会用了多元元素，这些不可调和、本身风格反差大的东西，很难想像它们怎能放在同一个空间里。我希望通过一个变异的方式来表现它们，既保存了物件本来的特征，又能通过差异挖掘出被隐藏的个性”。这多元的元素正好和上海对应。因为元素够多，所以想像也可以无限。上海和雍福会巧妙地成就了对方。要说装修的风格，这里可以说是没有风格，主人用色绮丽大胆，挥洒自如，自成风格，似乎更像是在演绎一场昔日遗梦，一场西方人眼中的华美中国旧梦。

“It is hard to imagine that all these conflicting and incompatible elements could be possibly put in the same space. I hope to present them in such a way that the original features are preserved while the hidden individuality can be excavate.” The multiple-culture of Yongfoo is exactly corresponding with the equally multiple-cultured Shanghai. The style of Yongfoo Elite is the style of its own where the designer does not follow any rule at all. He is bold in the color and free in his imagination as if he is trying to stage an old dream, a dream about the magnificent Chinese in the eyes of the Westerners.

“上海本来就是一个移民城市，包容了来自不同国家不同民族的多种文化。文化有独立的差异性，也有相互的影响。雍福会就是希望用现代人的想法来表现这一特殊的文化气质”。即使在开业半年以后，只要突然有一个新构想出来，汪兴政仍然会对任何一个细节稍有不满便推倒重来。

“Shanghai is a city of immigrants, a melting pot of different cultures of different nations and peoples. Cultures differ from and influence each other. Yongfoo Elite is such an example where such a special cultural trait is conveyed through modern thought.” Even half a year after Yongfoo’s opening, as long as he had hit upon a new idea, Wang Xingzheng would still do it once again.

“室内设计与其他设计是相通的，而且发挥的余地更广。我把雍福会当作一个试验。雍福会的试验性在于物质都有其本性，要从中找出性格特征，让不同物质相互吸收和认可。这可不是件容易的事情。除了有钱，还需要有品，有肚量。钱是一定要砸的，那是学费。单单六艺堂的3次拆装，就耗资上千万。但所有的失败都是必然的，失败也是学习的过程。没错，雍福会是

雍福会一角
a corner of Yongfoo Elite

一个商品，但我当时的唯一理想就是做成它。等到你真的做到极致了，得到的回报也是极致的。我一直确信，当我完成雍福会之后，它已经不是我的了。它属于上海，它与这个城市共存，跟我存在与否没有太大关系”。

“Interior design is the same as the design of other kinds, and it provides more room for imagination. Yongfoo Elite is my experiment. Yongfoo Elite is experimental in that you have to find out the personalities of the stuff and make them acknowledge and accept one another. This is not easy. You have got to have taste and generosity besides money. Money is a must because you have to pay to learn. The three-time reconstructions of Liu Yi Tang cost around ten million Yuan. But all the failures are inevitable and rewarding. It is true that Yongfoo Elite is a commodity. The only thing I thought then was to make it and make it well. When you finally make it, you will be enormously rewarded. I have always believed that from the moment of its completion, it is no longer mine. It belongs to Shanghai and has nothing to do with me.”

上海的使馆区最记得旧时的繁华，时过境迁倒愈发沉着安静起来，固守着什么似的，不与响亮摩登的商业区争风。在这条马路上的雍福会，就好像一个穿着旗袍的20世纪20年代上海女子，虽然包裹得严严实实，却依旧风情万种。这里也是喝下午茶绝好的地方，安安静静地在半露天的连廊看书，欣赏着好听的背景音乐，听着庭院里鸟声啼鸣，看着鱼池里金鱼悠闲地游来游去，吹着凉爽微风，看松柏与枫树相互映衬，就如自家的花园，不胜江南，却别有一种气韵。这样美好的意境真让人流连忘返。

The consular district used to be so prosperous and bustling. But as time goes by, it is getting quiet as if it is trying to stick to something. Yongfoo Elite on this road is just like a Shanghai girl in 1920s. Though tightly wrapped in cheongsam, her beauty shines from within. It is a perfect place for the afternoon tea. Reading in the corridor can be so inviting an experience,with the appealing music.The singing birds and the swimming fish. It is, though not as beautiful as the view in south China, of a unique flavor of its own.

夜间的雍福会也很美，从连廊回看小楼，暖色的灯从底下渐映在几株垂柳间，绿柳呈软玉色，滴滴随风。底下带状河中的肥大锦鲤遇光时明、潜水则暗。楼的整体隐去了，更有画意。

Yongfoo Elite at night is even more beautiful. With the warm light looming, the green willows are rendered bluish waving in the breeze. The fat fancy carp in the ribbon-like creek beneath are bright and dark at intervals corresponding to the light. With the building gradually disappearing in the dark, it is even more picturesque.

它如闹市中的桃花源，是某些圈子里的秘密，口口相传。来这里的人多是有所憧憬的，怀揣着各样追忆的心情。在雍福会消磨时光，兼有参观博物馆之感，或曰欣赏美学家暨古典收藏家的主人之富藏和感受历史的沧桑。既要动脑筋，还得用心记，看见“密训堂”匾额不必怕，看见“悬规”、“植矩”石匾，想一想，同“循规蹈矩”有何异同。而一个个国际名人由雍福会的小门走进去，带着一个夜晚的美好回忆入梦。

It is a Garden of Eden in the bustling city and also a secret in some social circles. People that come here are usually to pursue some kind of dream. Walking here among the collection of the owner might give you a better understanding about history. It is more than a place for leisure and entertainment; it is a place for thinking and wondering. All kinds of international celebrities walk in with a dream and come out with a beautiful memory .

老上海，是座记忆中的城，人人有个碎片拼缀起的华丽版本，却又无须再现些什么。留下来的，就一直在那儿了，转个弯，就会在街角遇见。

Old Shanghai is a city of memory. Everyone harbors a dream that is put together with pieces. What is left is still and will always be there, right around the corner.